Some Men
and
Deuce

Other works by Terrence McNally

Plays

And Things That Go Bump in the Night • *¡Cuba Si!* • *Next* • *Sweet Eros and Witness* • *Tour in "Collision Course"* • *Where Has Tommy Flowers Gone?* • *Whiskey* • *Bad Habits* • *The Ritz* • *It's Only a Play* • *Frankie and Johnny in the Clair de Lune* • *Faith, Hope, and Charity* • *The Lisbon Traviata* • *Lips Together, Teeth Apart* • *A Perfect Ganesh* • *Love! Valour! Compassion!* • *By the Sea, By the Sea, By the Beautiful Sea* • *Master Class* • *Five Short Plays* • *Corpus Christi* • *The Wibbly, Wobbly, Wiggly Dance That Cleopatterer Did* • *Full Frontal Nudity* • *Prelude & Liebestod* • *The Stendahl Syndrome* • *Dedication or The Stuff of Dreams* • *Some Men* • *Deuce* • *Unusual Acts of Devotion*

Musicals and Operas (librettos)

The Rink • *Kiss of the Spider Woman* • *Ragtime* • *The Full Monty* • *The Visit* • *A Man of No Importance* • *Chita Rivera: The Dancer's Life* • *Dead Man Walking*

Screenplays and Teleplays

Apple Pie • *The Five Forty-Eight* • *Mama Malone* • *Sam Found Out or The Queen of Mababawe (written with Wendy Wasserstein)* • *Andre's Mother* • *Trying Times II: L/S/M/F/T* • *Frankie and Johnny in the Clair de Lune* • *The Last Mile* • *Common Ground (Mr. Roberts)* • *The Ritz* • *Love! Valour! Compassion!*

TERRENCE McNALLY

Some Men
and
Deuce

Grove Press
New York

Published simultaneously in Canada
Printed in the United States of America

FIRST EDITION

ISBN: 978-0-8021-4449-2

Grove Press
an imprint of Grove/Atlantic, Inc.
841 Broadway
New York, NY 10003

Distributed by Publishers Group West

www.groveatlantic.com

09 10 11 12   10 9 8 7 6 5 4 3 2 1

For my spouse, Tom Kirdahy

CONTENTS

SOME MEN

Some Men was commissioned by Susan Dietz and Peter Schneider and developed by the Sundance Institute Theatre Program under the direction of Philip Himberg. The world premiere was produced by Philadelphia Theatre Company (Sara Garonzik, Producing Artistic Director).

Some Men received its New York premiere at Second Stage Theatre (Carole Rothman, Artistic Director; Ellen Richard, Executive Director; Christopher Burney, Associate Artistic Director) on March 26, 2007. It was directed by Trip Cullman; the set design was by Mark Wendland; the costume design was by Linda Cho; the lighting design was by Kevin Adams; the sound design was by John Gromada; the stage manager was Stephanie Gatton; the production stage manager was Lori Ann Zepp; and the production manager was Jeff Wild. The cast was as follows:

AARON/TOMMY'S DAD/BUFFED IN CHELSEA/ TREY/JOSEPH	Don Amendolia
BERNIE/MARTIN	Kelly AuCoin
CARL/XERXES/JOEL/KURT/GARY	Romain Frugé
MARTY/SCOOP/CAMUS/ARCHIE/"ROXIE"	David Greenspan
PERRY/BRAD/PADRAIC/BOYTOY/BJ/PAT/ SPENCER	Jesse Hooker
MARCUS/LESTER/THE SNAKE/ALEX/ANGEL EYES/ GORDON/SEB	Michael McElroy
FRITZ/MENDY/DAVID GOLDMAN/RANDY HUNK/ ZACH/LEWIS/MEL/NURSE JACK	Pedro Pascal
PIANO MAN/JACKSON/FUNERAL DIRECTOR/ DOWNTOWN I I/"MARY"/MR. KEYS/BUSBOY	Randy Redd
PAUL/DARREN/TOP DOG/CLIFF/WILL/MICHAEL/ DICK/RICHARD	Frederick Weller

ACT ONE

The Wedding

Darkness. We hear a man's voice, a cappella, singing. It is soon joined by other male voices. As the light begins to come up, we see two men dancing together. They are easy, confident, graceful together. As the singing gets louder, the men's dance becomes more intimate and romantic. As the lights come up to full, the two dancers separate and join the rest of the company. Music changes to a traditional wedding march. We are in attendance at a wedding. We watch the company follow the progression of the unseen wedding procession with their eyes. They are appropriately dressed for the occasion. One of them is in full U.S. Army parade dress. Now the actors face forward. We never see the wedding partners or the minister.

MARTY Uncle Archie would have loved this. The flowers, the music, the Waldorf-Astoria, for Christ's sake! Uncle Archie would have been one of the bridesmaids. No, Uncle Archie would have been the maid of honor—every Bethpage, Long Island, drag queen inch of him.

BERNIE Did you bring the envelope?

CARL No, you did.

BERNIE I hope that's a joke.

CARL It's not.

BERNIE Carl!

CARL What's the matter?

BERNIE I don't have it.

CARL Well neither do I.

BERNIE I told you I was leaving it on the kitchen counter.

CARL No one leaves wedding checks on the kitchen counter.

BERNIE I do.

CARL So now it's my fault.

BERNIE I didn't say that.

CARL The wedding check was your responsibility.

BERNIE Everything in this relationship is my responsibility.

MARTY Sssshhhhh.

BERNIE I hate you.

CARL Not half as much as I hate you right now.

MARTY Ssssshhhhh!

BERNIE The Bible is right: Two men living together is completely unnatural.

CARL That's not what it says but it should.

AARON When did I become the oldest person everywhere I go? Better question: When did I realize it?

PERRY Marcus, I can't tell if the minister is a man or a woman.

MARCUS You're not supposed to at these things, Perry. I think that's the point.

CARL (*to Perry*) We're not speaking.

PERRY (*to Marcus*) They're not speaking.

FRITZ I didn't know a wedding would be so cruise-y. I thought it would be all old men, like when you're in the Hamptons.

PERRY   I think that guy is cruising us, Marcus.

MARCUS   Don't flatter yourself, Perry. Did you give the babysitter our cell phones?

PAUL   First it was "Don't ask, don't tell." Now it's "I do." I'm very confused.

AARON   Friend of the groom?

PAUL   No, sir.

AARON   Friend of the other groom?

PAUL   No, sir. My friend Tommy was a friend of theirs. I'm here for him.

PERRY   Michael looks terrific.

MARCUS   Michael always looks terrific. I hate him.

VOICE   Dearly beloved. We are gathered here to celebrate the joyful union of two loving hearts: you, Michael, and you, Eugene, in the holy sacrament of marriage.

AARON   For better or for worse, in sickness and in health. I wonder if they know how profound those vows are? We did, Scoop. We were supposed to grow old together. Scoop and Aaron, Aaron and Scoop. 'Til death do us part. And it did. (*Aaron exits*)

PAUL   Some people think this marriage thing is going to be the end of gay life as it has been practiced on this planet for a hundred million years.

FRITZ   How do you mean?

MARTY   If we can get married we'll be like everyone else. (*Paul exits*)

FRITZ   Fat chance of that.

MARTY I'm fabulous. I want to stay fabulous.

FRITZ Go ahead. Who's stopping you?

Fritz and Marty exit.

PERRY There's nothing fabulous about not being able to visit your partner when he's in the E.R. on life support.

MARCUS Why am I always the one in the E.R. when you get on your soapbox? (*Perry and Marcus exit.*)

PIANO MAN I don't think much of the music they've chosen. Someone should write a gay "Sunrise, Sunset." They'd make a bundle.

The Piano Man exits. BERNIE and CARL are left alone onstage.

BERNIE I haven't been at the Waldorf in years. This used to be quite the place for very discreet assignations. The last time I was here I—

CARL Bernie, you are the only person on the planet who still uses the word assignations.

BERNIE That's what we called them.

Carl exits.

VOICE Knowing the joy that accompanies your love for one another and firmly believing in the fulfillment of a lifetime together, do you take each other to be spouses for life?

Bernie is left alone as we transition.

WALDORF HOTEL (1968)

ZACH *is kissing Bernie. It is quite a while before one of them breaks it off.*

BERNIE This is my first time, not that it matters.

ZACH First time with a man or first time with a man who knew what he was doing? (*Zach kisses him again.*)

BERNIE (*startled, turning*) Wait! I thought I heard something. Did you hear anything?

ZACH No. Traffic on Park Avenue, maids or room service in the hallway, nothing we have to worry about.

BERNIE I think hotels like the Waldorf-Astoria have house detectives.

ZACH For sure.

BERNIE That's all I need. A house detective at the door.

ZACH Not to worry: I slipped him a five.

BERNIE He knows what we're doing?

ZACH He couldn't care less. Most of them are gay anyway. He's a refugee from Castro. We're fine.

BERNIE I'm sorry, but I know someone who was entrapped.

ZACH Did he like it?

BERNIE Of course not, it was horrible. He lost his job, his wife left him.

ZACH I was making a joke.

BERNIE Not a very good one.

ZACH No, not a very good one. (*He starts to unbutton Bernie's shirt.*)

BERNIE I can do that.

ZACH I'm not going to let you.

BERNIE   These are especially dangerous times to be caught doing something like this. That damn World's Fair and Mayor Lindsay's ridiculous vice squads.

ZACH   Tell me about it! Lindsay just wants to get re-elected. They're a complete waste of everybody's time—theirs and ours. Put your arms over your head.

BERNIE   Have you had a bad experience?

ZACH   I was in a bar that got raided.

Zach has finished unbuttoning and has removed Bernie's shirt.

ZACH (*cont.*)   Put your arms over your head.

Bernie raises his arms over his head. Zach quickly strips him of his undershirt.

BERNIE   What happened?

ZACH   They took us in, booked us, made us pay a fine and take a solemn promise we'd never go in another gay bar again. You can put your arms down now.

BERNIE   I wondered what you were going to do. This really is my first time with a . . .

ZACH   I believe you. The word is hustler. I prefer escort. Actually, I prefer Zach.

BERNIE   Is that your real name?

ZACH   Nobody else's. Zachary. Zach.

BERNIE   My best friend at Dart—at college was a Zach.

ZACH   Did you two . . . ?

BERNIE No, no, nothing like that. I fooled around some in high school but once I got to college I decided I'd be better off fooling around with girls.

ZACH I can see that.

BERNIE How do you mean?

ZACH Your ring.

BERNIE Oh.

ZACH Are you?

BERNIE What?

ZACH Better off?

BERNIE No.

ZACH You have a nice chest, Bob.

BERNIE What? Oh! Thank you.

ZACH Most guys I do this with your age have weak bodies, all flab, even the skinny ones.

BERNIE I try to get to the New York Athletic Club once a week.

ZACH I can see that.

BERNIE I'm a squash man. You play squash?

ZACH No, but I've been taken to lunch at your club.

BERNIE By a member?

ZACH I clean up good, if I have to.

BERNIE I didn't know we had any gay members.

ZACH What are you?

BERNIE It's a really good workout, squash is. Keeps you very alert or you can get really wonked by the ball. I was out cold for five minutes once. They had to call an ambulance.

ZACH Can we concentrate on what we're doing?

BERNIE If you think I'm nervous, you're right.

ZACH Come here. You know that advertisement, "Leave the driving to us"?

BERNIE Yes?

Zach starts to undo the belt on Bernie's pants.

BERNIE (*cont.*) I can do that.

ZACH I told you, Bob, I'm not going to let you.

BERNIE What about you?

ZACH What about me?

BERNIE Aren't you going to undress?

ZACH Is the Pope Catholic?

BERNIE (*who's never heard this expression*) Yes.

His pants fall to his ankles.

ZACH Nice. I had you figured for boxers.

BERNIE You have more choices with boxers. I wasn't sure which to wear.

ZACH You chose fine. Step out of your trousers.

BERNIE You want my socks off, too?

ZACH Everything goes. You have great legs, Bob.

BERNIE   Thank you.

ZACH   It must be all that squash.

BERNIE   Let me hang these up. I've got to look sharp for a meeting.

ZACH   Cool scar. Where'd you get it?

BERNIE   Courtesy of Uncle Sam.

ZACH   You served?

BERNIE   Yes.

ZACH   *Why?*

BERNIE   We didn't have much choice.

ZACH   Sure you did.

BERNIE   I wasn't doing this then. Besides, I believed in what we were fighting for. But *this* war.

ZACH   I hate it. I'm glad they don't want us. I'd head for Canada before I let them take me.

BERNIE   You a New Yorker?

ZACH   Texas.

BERNIE   What brought you to the Big Apple?

ZACH   I'm a junior at Columbia.

BERNIE   That's a good school.

ZACH   I know.

BERNIE   What are you majoring in?

ZACH   English. Take off your shorts.

BERNIE   English? Me, too. How did you get to Columbia all the way from Texas?

ZACH   I had a fantastic high school English teacher. I went from my graduation directly to the Greyhound bus station.

BERNIE   How did you get into this?

ZACH   It's a long story.

BERNIE   I'd like to hear it.

ZACH   For seventy-five dollars all you get is fantastic sex with an English major on a paltry scholarship who has a paper on Milton to write tonight. Now take your shorts off.

BERNIE   Could we get the money part over now? Afterward, I'm going to feel, I don't know . . . Can I turn off some lights?

ZACH   Sure. Take off your shorts, Bob.

BERNIE   My name's not Bob. I feel weird every time you say it.

ZACH   Take off your shorts, whoever you are.

BERNIE   It's Bernie.

ZACH   Take off your shorts, Bernie.

Bernie takes off his shorts.

ZACH (*cont.*)   Again, you're a man of surprises.

BERNIE   I'm not feeling very sexy.

ZACH   It's okay. We got all night.

BERNIE   We said one hour.

ZACH   I'm not looking at the clock.

BERNIE I love my wife but sometimes I get these urges to be with a man so bad I think I'm gonna go crazy. I'm so tired of jacking off in our bathroom with Susan on the other side of the door in our bedroom. I want to go Yow! when I come, once, just once in my life, go Yow! and mean it. I want the whole world to hear me when I come. I want me to hear me.

ZACH You've never gone yow?

BERNIE It's more like a yeep.

ZACH Take off the ring, Bernie.

BERNIE I. I'd rather not.

ZACH You want the whole world to hear you, don't you?

BERNIE Yes.

ZACH Bernie, take off the ring.

Bernie takes off his ring. Zach pulls his own shirt off. Then his pants.

ZACH (*cont.*) Is this okay?

BERNIE Yes.

Bernie has begun to softly cry.

ZACH You want me to be active or passive? I can do both. I prefer active. Look at me, Bernie. Stop crying and look at me.

Bernie looks at Zach.

ZACH (*cont.*) What's it going to be?

Lights go down on them. Transition.

THANK YOU FOR COMING (2007)

One of the men of the company steps forward and plays "Taps." At its conclusion, TOMMY'S DAD *is seen sitting apart. He is wearing his U.S. Army veteran's uniform.* PAUL *approaches and salutes him. He is in his Iraqi uniform which he was wearing at the wedding but this time he is on crutches.*

PAUL Sir . . . ?

TOMMY'S DAD Yes?

PAUL Tom's dad?

TOMMY'S DAD Yes?

PAUL I was a friend of Tommy's.

TOMMY'S DAD Oh.

PAUL We were in the same unit.

TOMMY'S DAD I see.

PAUL I wanted to be here today.

TOMMY'S DAD At ease, soldier.

PAUL I just made it.

TOMMY'S DAD All the way from . . . ?

PAUL Yes, sir.

TOMMY'S DAD Kirkuk? Am I saying it right? Kirkuk?

PAUL Yes, sir, Kirkuk.

TOMMY'S DAD Funny name for a place. I suppose Poughkeepsie is, too, if you think about it. Names! That's a long flight.

PAUL Yes, sir, it is. Twenty-six hours. We changed planes in Germany.

TOMMY'S DAD Dusseldorf.

PAUL Yes, sir. Got off one plane and right onto another.

TOMMY'S DAD We've got that big base there. Leap-frogging, they used to call it.

PAUL They still do, sir.

TOMMY'S DAD I said "at ease," son. My look is worse than my bite.

PAUL Thank you, sir.

TOMMY'S DAD I didn't serve overseas. I think the Army decided drilling fresh recruits was all I was good for. They sent me to the Canal Zone once. Didn't much care for it. Tommy was the traveler in the family. Always going somewhere, doing something different. The Army was his ticket to the big world out there. Not much for him here. A restless boy.

PAUL Yes, sir. I brought you this.

He hands Tommy's dad the battalion flag.

PAUL (*cont.*) It's the . . .

TOMMY'S DAD I know the drill. They give the parents a flag. Or the wife. But most of these boys are so young they didn't have time to marry. I asked Tommy when he was going to get married and he said he hadn't found the right girl. I told him, "Maybe you have, son, and just don't know it yet." Are you married?

PAUL No, sir.

TOMMY'S DAD Girlfriend?

PAUL No, sir.

TOMMY'S DAD Sometimes I think they're more trouble than they're worth, women are. Thank you for coming, soldier.

PAUL It's Paul. Please, I'd like you to call me Paul.

TOMMY'S DAD Paul! You're the friend Tommy went to . . .

PAUL Hawaii with. Yes, sir.

TOMMY'S DAD He said you had a room right on a beach and you could jump into the ocean anytime you wanted.

PAUL Yes, sir, we did.

TOMMY'S DAD That must have been a nice break from . . .

PAUL Yes, sir, it was.

TOMMY'S DAD Tell me something: Did Tommy ever kill anyone?

PAUL I don't know, sir. I don't think so.

TOMMY'S DAD I can't imagine Tommy ever killing someone.

PAUL He would have if he'd had to. He wasn't a sissy.

TOMMY'S DAD I'm not suggesting he was. You know the thing that angers me? The thing I can never forgive? Tommy never met that special person.

PAUL Maybe he did, sir.

TOMMY'S DAD You can't keep a secret like that.

PAUL It's not that a person keeps a secret so much as they don't think another person wants to hear it.

TOMMY'S DAD   Maybe Tommy's secrets are in this flag and maybe they should stay there.

PAUL   Tommy didn't have secrets.

TOMMY'S DAD   Everyone has secrets, Paul.

PAUL   Secrets they shouldn't have to keep.

The FUNERAL DIRECTOR *quietly goes up to them.*

FUNERAL DIRECTOR   I'm sorry but we're beginning and this row is for the immediate family.

TOMMY'S DAD   Thank you for coming, young man.

PAUL   Would you . . . ? Could I . . . ?

They embrace awkwardly.

PAUL (*cont.*)   Thank you, sir.

TOMMY'S DAD   Did that help?

PAUL   Everything helps.

TOMMY'S DAD   Sit in the row behind us. If anyone says anything, tell them you're a friend of the family.

PAUL   Thank you, sir.

TOMMY'S DAD   I can't give you what you want, young man.

PAUL   I loved your son.

Transition.

SUR LA MER I (1922)

Night. We hear a pounding surf. DAVID GOLDMAN *and* PADRAIC *run on. They have been swimming.*

DAVID   I'm freezing. Aren't you cold? I've got some brandy. We'll make a fire.

PADRAIC   I'm used to colder. This is nothing. The Irish Sea is so cold me cock fell off. They had to send a search party out to find it. Lucky for me, they did.

DAVID   Lucky for both of us. I've never gone in the ocean this early. Nobody goes in until the Fourth in East Hampton—and sometimes not even then. Here, I'll dry your back.

PADRAIC   Thank you, Mr. Goldman.

DAVID   How many times do I have to tell you: I don't want you to call me Mr. Goldman when we're alone like this.

PADRAIC   What about when I'm chauffeuring that new Packard of yours and you got some debutante in the back seat and you're heading to the opera house?

DAVID   That's different. But when we're in bed and you say, "I'm coming, Mr. Goldman! I'm coming!" it puts me right off what we're doing.

PADRAIC   To tell you the truth, it puts me off a bit, too, sir.

DAVID   No "sir" either!

PADRAIC   Next time, I promise, it'll be, "I'm coming, David! I'm coming, I'm coming, I'm coming!"

DAVID   You'll wake the whole beach!

He clasps his hand over Padraic's mouth. They look deep into each other's eyes.

DAVID (*cont.*)   Will you be good now?

He takes his hand off Padraic's mouth.

PADRAIC (*softly*)   David, David, David.

DAVID   That wasn't so hard, was it?

PADRAIC   Then will you stop calling me your Danny Boy?

DAVID   It's affectionate.

PADRAIC   It's fecking ridiculous. You do it all the time. Ask Liam.

DAVID   Who's Liam?

PADRAIC   The lad in the elevator at your apartment house. We laugh at you behind your back, we do.

DAVID   Is he...?

PADRAIC   What?

DAVID   Liam, is he like you...?

PADRAIC   Like me? Why? You fancy him now?

DAVID   Of course not.

PADRAIC   You think all Irishmen are queer? It's against our religion.

DAVID   It's against all religions.

PADRAIC   Feck all they know about it. The first man who put his hand on me cock was a priest.

DAVID   What did you do?

PADRAIC   Nothing, I loved it. You gotta love the Catholic Church! Give me a cigarette, will you?

They sit and smoke.

DAVID   Are you tired?

PADRAIC Not after that swim.

DAVID You worked hard today.

PADRAIC We both did.

DAVID I like looking at the house from here. All the windows glowing softly. I'm glad we got it up and running early this season.

PADRAIC We're still not done.

DAVID I have it planned: We're not going to be finished for a good week. I have you all to myself out here. The stock exchange will just have to do without me.

PADRAIC Your father is going to have something to say about that.

DAVID My father can go to hell and take his bank with him. I'm a different man when I'm with you. I could dance right now. Dance like I didn't have a care in the world. Dance in the moonlight like a crazy pagan person.

PADRAIC Go ahead, I'm not stopping you. I could use a good laugh.

DAVID May I kiss you?

PADRAIC Only on the mouth. None of your cheeky, necky kisses, David.

They kiss.

PADRAIC (*cont.*) You knew right off about me, didn't you? That this was going to happen?

DAVID I wasn't sure.

PADRAIC Put your hand out.

Padraic burns David with his cigarette.

PADRAIC (*cont.*)   Didn't that hurt?

DAVID   Of course it hurt.

PADRAIC   You didn't act like it hurt.

DAVID   I didn't want to give you the satisfaction.

PADRAIC   You hurt me, you'll know.

DAVID   I don't want to hurt you.

PADRAIC   That's because you can't. I'm tough. Why do you call the house Sur La Mer, David?

DAVID   Because it's on the ocean.

PADRAIC   Call it that then. On the ocean! Sur La Mer! You're not French, are you?

DAVID   I've never met anyone like you.

PADRAIC   Go over to the West Forties, Hell's Kitchen, one night. There's a dozen like me on every corner.

DAVID   I want to spend as much of my life with you as I can.

PADRAIC   You're a bigger dreamer than I thought, Mr. Goldman.

DAVID   David.

PADRAIC   David until we're back in town and your mother asks you when you're going to get married and your father sees me standing there in my chauffeur's uniform with me cap in me hand like some Irish sod and he tells me the car needs washing and you look at me like you don't know me and I'm back to calling you Mr. Goldman again.

DAVID   We're the only ones who have to know!

PADRAIC   Truth is, I prefer "Mr. Goldman" to "David." I know my place. I hate it but I know it.

DAVID   Your place is with me.

PADRAIC   Right now, being here like this . . .

DAVID   What, Padraic, what?

PADRAIC   A part of me believes you.

DAVID   I am so happy when I am with you.

PADRAIC   Then I think of me mother working eighteen hours a day, on her knees, scrubbing up people like your's slop, and I hate you all over again.

DAVID   I didn't make the world this way.

PADRAIC   If there weren't this electricity between us …

DAVID   You feel it, too?

PADRAIC   I'd have killed you by now.

Padraic's hands are around David's throat.

DAVID   Do it, go on, do it, right here on this beach.

PADRAIC   Would you like that, David?

DAVID   I'll wash up on some distant shore and everyone will wonder where I came from.

Padraic takes his hands from David's throat but only after a long time of keeping them there.

PADRAIC   Do you remember what you said the first time you saw me dressed in my chauffeur's uniform?

DAVID I love you, Padraic.

PADRAIC No, you said, "You're late. Your boots are scuffed. Don't just stand there, bring the car around." And I did.

Transition.

INTERNET (2004)

The men are sitting apart at their computer keyboards. They are on the Internet and "talking" to each other in a "chat" room.

XERXES Heads up, chat room. UWS SCORPIO is not honest about his HIV status.

BOYTOY UWS?

XERXES Upper West Side, Boy Toy.

BOYTOY Thanks, Xerxes, I'm new to New York.

XERXES Welcome. He's a real asshole.

BOYTOY People misrepresent themselves on here?

XERXES Out and out lie is more like it.

BUFFED IN CHELSEA Hi, Boytoy. Buffed in Chelsea here. I'm 6'2", handsome, versatile. Told I look like something out of a Calvin Klein catalogue.

XERXES Sears Roebuck is more like it. If you like 'em fat and fifty, he's all yours, Boytoy!

BUFFED IN CHELSEA Xerxes? I thought you'd signed off.

XERXES Give it a rest, Buffed in Chelsea.

CAMUS There's usually more people online than this. It must be the weather. LOL!

MICHAEL   LOL, Camus?

CAMUS   Laughing out loud, Top Dog.

MICHAEL   Funny, I couldn't hear you!

CAMUS   LOL!

MICHAEL   You LOL a lot, Camus.

CAMUS   I'm a happy guy. You want to go into a private chat?

MICHAEL   Why?

CAMUS   I prefer privacy when I chat. I don't believe in casting my pearls before swine, know what I mean?

MICHAEL   Not everyone in the chat room is a swine.

CAMUS   But some of us are pearls. Here goes! I'm in. Are you?

MICHAEL   Yes.

CAMUS   Hi, Top Dog.

MICHAEL   Hi, Camus.

CAMUS   So what are you wearing?

MICHAEL   Sorry, not interested.

CAMUS   That was a joke.

MICHAEL   Not interested.

CAMUS   If you had heard the inflection in my voice, I think you would have been amused.

MICHAEL   N.I.!

CAMUS   N.I.?

MICHAEL   Not Interested!

CAMUS   Humor doesn't travel on the Internet. At least my kind of humor doesn't.

MICHAEL   You got that right.

CAMUS   Can I call you? So you can hear me say, "What are you wearing?"

MICHAEL   I'm wearing nothing but a cartridge belt and carrying an Uzi. I'm armed with several very sharp hunting knives and a sledgehammer. I'm listening to Wagner and celebrating Hitler's birthday. I voted for both Bushes both times. When I log off, I'm going to sodomize an eight-year-old Cub Scout.

CAMUS   You are getting me so hot, Top Dog. Now I really want to meet you.

MICHAEL   You're fucking sick, man.

CAMUS   That was another joke.

MICHAEL   *NOT INTERESTED!* Bold, italics, underlined, all caps.

CAMUS   You already said that.

MICHAEL   I have a small vocabulary.

CAMUS   That's all right, you have a big dick.

MICHAEL   Who told you that?

CAMUS   Your profile. You're eight inches. Cut.

MICHAEL   I am. You?

CAMUS   It also says you live in Manhattan, you weigh one hundred and seventy-three pounds, you're 6'1" and slightly receding. (I liked that, "slightly receding.") You're looking for a long-term relationship and you have a dog. The last book you read was the Bible and your motto is *carpe diem,* which you had the good taste not to translate.

MICHAEL   I asked you a question.

CAMUS   I'm a healthy six. And a half. My name is Kennie by the way. You don't have to give me yours. I sort of like Top Dog.

MICHAEL   Cut?

CAMUS   I am usually a bottom and enjoy anal sex provided my partner is wearing a rubber. Uncut. Was the last book you read really the Bible?

MICHAEL   My name is Michael. Yes.

CAMUS   That's amazing!

MICHAEL   What is?

CAMUS   The last book *I* read was the Bible.

MICHAEL   Fuck you.

CAMUS   No, really.

MICHAEL   Asshole.

CAMUS   Why don't you believe me? For all I know, the last book *you* read was a comic book and your dick is three inches.

MICHAEL   Really?

CAMUS   What really?

MICHAEL   The last book you read was the Bible?

CAMUS   I swear on it.

MICHAEL   Why?

CAMUS   Probably for the same reasons you did. I mean, there's got to be more to life than surfing the Internet at 2 A.M. on a Saturday night and telling total strangers we have ten inches.

MICHAEL   Was that a put-down?

CAMUS   No! I hate the Internet sometimes.

MICHAEL   I really do have eight inches. I hear you, man.

CAMUS   I like you calling me "man." I felt a connection.

MICHAEL   Connections are good.

CAMUS   They're all we have! Let me call you.

MICHAEL   I'm not comfortable with that.

CAMUS   I just want to hear what you sound like.

MICHAEL   I sound like this. LOL! (*He leaves his computer and exits the stage.*)

CAMUS   You want to call me?

Long pause.

CAMUS (*cont.*)   You still there?

Another long pause.

CAMUS (*cont.*)   "Only connect."

MICHAEL *returns to his computer and reads* CAMUS' *message and types.*

MICHAEL   E.M. Forster, right?

CAMUS Right. I had a boyfriend.

MICHAEL Had?

CAMUS AIDS.

MICHAEL I'm sorry.

CAMUS We were together eleven years. His father told him he hoped he got it.

MICHAEL Fathers are cunts.

CAMUS But I'm negative. Mine isn't.

MICHAEL Ditto. Isn't what?

CAMUS A cunt. I get tested every two months.

MICHAEL Every three.

CAMUS Have you lost someone?

MICHAEL Not like you.

THE SNAKE Need a pair of tickets for Madonna at the Garden Saturday.

BUFFED IN CHELSEA Lots of luck, Snake.

BOYTOY She sold out in two hours.

DOWNTOWN II Anyone looking to PNP?

BOYTOY What's PNP, Downtown 11?

BUFFED IN CHELSEA He's looking to score some crystal.

THE SNAKE Madonna tix? S.O.S. Madonna at the Garden.

CAMUS I know another person shouldn't be the answer to our questions about life but it's awfully nice when they are. Happy hearts don't make questioning minds.

FRITZ I guess they don't. How old are you?

CAMUS Forty-six. When Matthew died one of our best friends told me, "Face it, Kennie, you've had your last cookie. There aren't anymore where he came from."

MICHAEL That's a shitty thing to say.

CAMUS I know. How old are you?

MICHAEL Tell me how you came to read the Bible.

THE SNAKE Will do anything for Madonna tickets. Desperate.

BUFFED IN CHELSEA How desperate, Snake?

THE SNAKE Not *that* desperate, Buffed in Chelsea.

CAMUS There's a church where I live. I walk by it several times a day. One day I noticed what was written over the door. "Son, observe the time and fly from Evil."

MICHAEL I love that passage.

CAMUS It was like a bolt of lightning. I couldn't get the words out of my head. "Son, observe the time and fly from Evil." It was like a father was talking to me. I was the son and the evil was what my life had become since Matthew died and time was running out. Obviously these words came from the Bible—

MICHAEL Ecclesiastes 4:23. I know them well.

CAMUS —and I began to read it to find out if there were more of them. There were, of course.

MICHAEL So many, so many, I know!

CAMUS But there was something more, too. There were stories of loss but there were stories of hope, as well.

MICHAEL   Both Testaments, absolutely, I hear you, man.

CAMUS   There were good people and there were bad people and there were people like me.

MICHAEL   Neither good nor bad, but hurt and bewildered and hungry for something more in their lives.

CAMUS   More than their pain and loneliness.

MICHAEL   And they found it in God's love.

CAMUS   And I realized I would find it, too, if I just let all the goodness, all the abundance of this world into my life again. And I have, Top Dog, I have.

MICHAEL   Where is this church?

CAMUS   Brooklyn. Park Slope.

MICHAEL   That where you are now?

CAMUS   Yes. You?

MICHAEL   Hell's Kitchen.

CAMUS   Is that going to be a deal-breaker? LOL! No problem, Top Dog, I can come to you.

A light has come up on FRITZ [*Randy Hunk*] *sitting at his computer.*

FRITZ   I like your profile, Top Dog.

MICHAEL   What do you like about it?

FRITZ   You play rough.

MICHAEL   Let me check yours, Randy Hunk.

CAMUS   What train are you near? I can take the N or R. Or the F or the 2 or the 3.

MICHAEL I like yours, too. Let me get rid of someone. Done. What do you get into?

FRITZ A little pain, a little rapture, a little bare-backing.

MICHAEL I hear you.

FRITZ Chemistry.

MICHAEL I love chemistry. You got any leather?

CAMUS Or I can catch a cab. Give me an address and I'm on my way.

MICHAEL So.

FRITZ I just noticed what time it is. Is the phone gonna work for you?

MICHAEL Absolutely. So.

FRITZ So.

MICHAEL I'm Michael.

FRITZ Fritz.

MICHAEL What are you wearing, Fritz?

AOL SUPERVISOR Top Dog is blocking your instant messages, Camus.

Camus stops typing. He sits at his keyboard. The lights fade slowly on Michael and Fritz as they work at their respective keyboards. The other men continue to type. The sounds of keyboards clicking are coming louder and faster now.

BUFFED IN CHELSEA Cool profile, Camus. Check me out.

*The lights fade on BUFFED IN CHELSEA still typing.
Transition.*

AT THE N.Y.A.C. (1971)

Bernie and WILL *are in the middle of a two-martini lunch in the main dining room. They are dressed in suits and ties. So are the other diners. A young* BUSBOY *is working nearby.*

WILL   Jesus, Bernie will you look at the rear end on that kid! He's worth dropping a fork just to watch him bend over again. Whoever does the hiring for the New York Athletic Club dining room, you gotta love him.

BERNIE   I'm going to leave Susan, Will.

WILL   You two have another fight?

BERNIE   No. We haven't had a fight in months but I've made a decision—calmly and finally this time. I'm going to tell her. I've already taken an apartment on West Seventy-fourth Street.

WILL   I hope you can get your deposit back. You're not leaving Susan, Bernie. Or keep it for a fuck pad. I'll go in on it with you. I'm tired of getting the fish-eye at the Waldorf. Waiter!

BERNIE   I'm serious, Will.

WILL   Have you ever been on the West Side, Bernie? I hope your Spanish is good.

BUSBOY   Yes, sir?

WILL   We'd like another round.

BUSBOY   I'm not your waiter. I'm the busboy. I'll tell him.

WILL   Well you should be a waiter. You've got too much on the ball to be a busboy. What's your name?

BUSBOY Nick.

WILL I'll put in a good word for you, Nick. (*He drops his fork.*) Oops.

BUSBOY I'll get it.

WILL Thank you, Nick.

Busboy retrieves Will's fork.

BUSBOY I'll get another one.

WILL These are Stoli's with zero-*nada-rien* vermouth.

BUSBOY Right away, sir.

He goes.

WILL I think Nick's gay. If he's not, he will be. Five will get you ten he's an actor, he's from the great Midwest and he knows his way around this particular block.

BERNIE Some of them are a little more than your pedestrian profile, Will.

WILL You think he takes it up the ass?

BERNIE I'm sorry. I thought I could talk to you about this.

WILL Ever since I gave you the number of that escort service you've been weird. You're supposed to fuck them, Bernie, not fall in love with them. Think with your head instead of your dick. You are married to a beautiful, wonderful woman. So you're not "happy," whatever that means. So what? Life isn't about being happy. It's about doing the right thing and the right thing for men like us is staying married and beaming with pride when our kids graduate from Yale or Harvard or wherever the fuck it is they want to go and enjoying our many grandchildren and the fruits of retirement. And I mean fruits in the traditional meaning of the word 'cause by then we'll both be too old to make ya-ya with anyone of either sex.

BERNIE   It wasn't an easy decision.

WILL   It was insane.

Indicating someone at another table.

WILL (*cont.*)   There's Gilbert Roberts. Can you hear his mouth if he knew what we were talking about? We wouldn't just be out of the club, he'd have us both drummed out of the city! Why are you telling me this and spoiling a perfectly good lunch?

BERNIE   You're one of my best friends.

WILL   No, I'm not. We have something in common. We're both family men who like a little recreation on the side. Take that away from the equation and I don't even particularly like you. You're moody, you're a lousy squash partner and you're a Democrat. But we both play a potentially dangerous game very neat and very safe. I look out for you and I expect the same from you. Nobody's looking to fall in love. Nobody gets hurt. It's our little secret. It's no skin off anybody's nose including Sue and Ellen. You think we're the only men in Manhattan who get a little something on the side? Grow up, wise up, Bernie. Jesus, I feel my lunch coming up on me.

BERNIE   Susan found some magazines.

WILL   Jesus, you mean jack-off stuff?

BERNIE   It was pretty explicit.

WILL Jesus Christ! I should move my stash.

BERNIE We tried some therapy with a shrink.

WILL What did he say?

BERNIE He said that I was sick, that I needed help.

WILL He's right. If you're thinking of doing this, you do.

BERNIE I don't believe I'm sick, Will. I've tried all my life to make it stop. I'm tired of fighting it.

WILL There's nothing to fight. Fuck your head off. Take some hustler with you when you go to Rome next month. Just don't make a public spectacle of yourself. What's Susan gonna do? Divorce you? Women don't care that much. Give it to her once a month and she'll be fine. I haven't fucked Ellen in six months. I don't think she's even noticed I haven't.

BERNIE I want to wake up in the morning and not dread the day and what's to come. I want to love the person next to me as fully and completely as I tried to love Susan. When I make love I want it to be an expression of who I am and not who I think I should be.

WILL That's so fucking pitiful it makes me sick. Tell me something, Bernie, man to man: Has it really been that much of an ordeal to fuck your wife these last ten years?

BERNIE Hey, come on. Don't talk like that, not about Susan.

WILL It's a good word. We both know what it means.

BERNIE It was never an ordeal. Never. Not once.

WILL Was it ever a pleasure?

BERNIE No.

WILL You are one fucked-up son of a bitch, Bernie.

BERNIE I know. That's why I'm doing this.

WILL You're just going to tell her you're homosexual?

BERNIE I don't think that's the issue, not after the magazines. I'm telling her I think we'll both be better off apart.

WILL You better not tell her about me!

BERNIE Of course not.

WILL Both our wives think we're best friends. If my wife says anything she got from Susan, I'll kill you, Bernie. I will track you down wherever you and some hustler are holed up and I will kill you with my two bare hands. I'm not going to let you destroy my life because you've decided to destroy yours. It's all this "gay is good" crap out there in the air all of a sudden. Gay is not good. Gay is loneliness and secrecy and a lifetime of shame. Gay sucks but they don't tell you that. They only tell you the good stuff you have with the twenty-year-old twinkie. They don't tell you about the ostracism, the jokes behind your back at the office. They don't tell you what it does to your career. They don't tell you what it does to your parents. It will kill them, Bernie. They don't tell you what it does to your kids. Do you honestly think they'll ever want to lay eyes on you again when they find out their father is just another faggot cocksucker? I feel sorry for you. Don't come running to me. Don't even come near me ever again. I don't know you after this. We are closed. Waiter! You asshole. You stupid fucking asshole. Waiter!

BUSBOY I'm not your waiter. I'll get him.

WILL Put it on my bill. (*He gets up.*) Goodbye, Bernie.

Transition.

STONEWALL (1969)

A piano bar off Sheridan Square. Show tunes are being sung by the patrons. CLIFF, TREY, BJ, JOEL *and* ALEX *sit around the piano and vigorously join in the merriment. Distant sounds of a protest taking place on the other side of Seventh Avenue can be heard from time to time during the scene that follows. The pianist ("MARY") finishes a rousing chorus with a flourish and general approbation.*

CLIFF (*to Mary*) Do you know "I Love A Cop"? It's from *Fiorello*—the first musical to win the Pulitzer Prize. I love, love, love the score of *Fiorello*.

TREY *Of Thee I Sing* was the first musical to win the Pulitzer Prize.

MARY He's right.

CLIFF All right, it's from the *second* musical to win the Pulitzer Prize. I still love, love, love it.

TREY Actually, it's the third. *South Pacific* was the second.

Mary plays a few bars of something from Fiorello. *Two men, Cliff and BJ, start dancing together to it.* MARTIN, *the bartender, quickly puts a stop to it.*

MARTIN Hey! Knock it off, BJ!

BJ We were hardly touching.

MARTIN Some cop comes in here and sees that and I get closed.

BJ Yadda yadda yadda. It's a fucking gulag.

MARTIN Tell your boyfriend I don't make the rules, Cliff. You want to know what a gulag is, go to England. What do you think I'm doing in this country? You boys don't know how lucky you are. This round is on me in memory of Judy Garland.

CLIFF I love, love, love Judy Garland.

TREY A moment of silence please for Judy. Thank you.

Different music begins. Joel and Alex have taken their drinks and moved apart from the others.

JOEL She looked so beautiful this morning. I'm glad we stood in line to see her. Campbell's did an amazing job.

ALEX It couldn't have been easy.

JOEL She was so lifelike. It was like she was sleeping. I wanted to touch her.

ALEX I couldn't believe when I read she was only forty-seven. I thought she was at least in her sixties.

JOEL And to think she never won an Oscar. I hate Hollywood.

ALEX I think she won a special children's Oscar.

JOEL Children's Oscars don't count.

ALEX You know who I feel sorry for? Joey. Liza and Lorna are gonna be fine. They have talent. But Joey! Can you imagine being Judy Garland's son?

JOEL   I used to fantasize about it. I saved her from herself.

ALEX   How did you do that?

JOEL   I just loved her so, so much.

ALEX   I wonder if she ever knew how much people loved her.

JOEL   Even straight people.

ALEX   But not like us.

JOEL   No, not like us.

ALEX   What are we going to do?

JOEL   Channel 13 is showing *A Star is Born* at midnight.

ALEX   I meant with the rest of our lives?

JOEL   I almost think you're serious.

Sounds of a rally from offstage.

JOEL *(cont.)*   We're not going anywhere with that going on. It's worth your life crossing Seventh Avenue. Martin, more peanuts!

MARTIN   The deed is servant to the wish.

JOEL   Don't you Brits ever age, Martin?

MARTIN   Age cannot wither, nor custom stale our infinite variety. Here you are, my hardies.

JOEL   Thanks, petal. What are they yelling out there? "Out of the what"?

MARTIN   Out of the closets and into the streets.

JOEL   What for?

MARTIN   I don't know. Ask them.

ALEX   Ssshh, listen a sec! Is that from *House of Flowers*?

JOEL   You think everything's from *House of Flowers*. Mary, what's that from?

MARY   *House of Flowers*.

Alex sticks his tongue out at Joel.

ALEX   Look at that one, at the end of the bar.

JOEL   I could hardly fail to notice him. He's gorgeous.

ALEX   He's a hustler.

JOEL   You think everyone's a hustler.

ALEX   At our age, almost everyone is. He's coming over.

Zach joins them. He is wearing a Columbia T-shirt.

ZACH   My friends and I thought maybe you could answer a question for us. Who replaced Shirley MacLaine after she replaced Carol Haney in *Pajama Game*?

JOEL   I don't know.

ZACH   Sorry, you looked like a couple of old show queens over here.

ALEX   We are a couple of old show queens. I'm Alex, he's Joel.

ZACH   Zachary, Zach. Hi.

ALEX   What are you reading?

ZACH   John Milton. *Paradise Lost*.

ALEX   I hated Milton in college.

JOEL   Everyone hates Milton, Alex.

ZACH   I don't.

ALEX   What are you drinking, Zachary?

ZACH   No, thanks. I'm getting ready to split and join the rally.

JOEL   We saw them. What are they rallying for?

ZACH   It started with the drag queens at the Stonewall protesting another raid but it's turning into a bunch of other things, too—mainly for the police to stop harassing us. My roommate was arrested on the piers Saturday night. Now his parents know, they're hassling him at work, his life is ruined.

JOEL   What was he doing?

ZACH   He was getting fucked.

JOEL   Well, no wonder.

ZACH   The cops cuffed him and beat the shit out of him.

JOEL   Which pier? I know some queens who would love to be cuffed and beaten.

ZACH   You think that's funny?

JOEL   No, but it is against the law.

ZACH   What is?

JOEL   Public fornication. Fucking.

ZACH   So are a lot of things that shouldn't be.

JOEL   *Men* fucking.

ZACH *No* fucking should be illegal. Straight people do it all the time.

JOEL In the privacy of their bedrooms. This was in a public place.

ZACH It was pitch dark.

JOEL That's not the point.

ZACH Have you ever been to the piers?

JOEL Not for your purposes.

ZACH What is your problem, mister?

JOEL The piers are private property.

ZACH Whose side are you on? You think it's okay to bust us just for being gay?

JOEL I think they should arrest us when we break the law.

ZACH The law is fucked up and so are you.

ALEX (*suddenly*) Nancy Bigelow! The actress who replaced Shirley MacLaine in *Pajama Game* was Nancy Bigelow.

ZACH Thanks. (*He is going.*)
Her name was Nancy Bigelow! (Assholes.) (*He is gone.*)

JOEL Nancy Bigelow. How did you know that?

ALEX I didn't. I just made it up. He was starting to annoy me. They're so strident, those people. They're going to ruin it for everyone else. What are you having?

JOEL I'm fine.

ALEX I can tell you're not. Neither of us is. Two martinis, Martin.

MARTIN Gin?

ALEX Yes, gin. Of course, gin. What else is there in a martini but gin? (*to Joel*) I honestly think vodka is responsible for the generation gap.

JOEL Judy drank vodka.

ALEX Judy drank everything. You wait, they're going to blame all this on her.

JOEL I still wish Judy had done the movie of *Gypsy* with Marilyn as Louise. I'm sure they'd have at least five minutes of usable footage by now. Now what's the matter?

ALEX Look at us, Joel. We're everything I never wanted to be: two queens sitting around in a bar listening to show tunes and talking about Judy Garland.

A drag queen [ARCHIE] has entered the bar and is waiting to be served.

ARCHIE Bartender. Oh Mr. Barkeep! Who do I have to fuck to get a drink in this preppy-ridden, show-tune-singing, aging queens motherfucking rat trap?

MARTIN We don't serve unescorted women.

ARCHIE I'm not a woman, you Cockney cretin. I'm a thirsty motherfucking drag queen. What are you looking at, Barbarella?

CLIFF Nothing.

ARCHIE You, too, Mary Poppins.

BJ No problem, buddy, to each his own.

TREY Ignore her. Attention's all they want.

ARCHIE I know my constitutional rights.

MARTIN This is a gay bar, mister.

ARCHIE No! All these men are gay?

MARTIN We serve men. You want to drink here? Dress like a man.

ARCHIE I'll dress any fucking way I fucking want. Who are you to fucking tell me how to fucking dress? If I want to fucking look like a woman, fucking walk like a woman and fucking fuck like a woman, then I fucking well want to fucking drink like a woman, you fucking illegal alien!

MARTIN I've got a green card.

ARCHIE I've got a green pussy.

MARTIN You want me to call the bouncer? Rusty!

Joel joins Archie at the bar.

JOEL The lady is with me, Martin. What are you having?

ARCHIE Thank you. Nothing fancy, rum and Coke.

JOEL That's Bacardi, Martin!

MARTIN I know!

JOEL You got to keep an eye on that one or he'll serve you rotgut.

ARCHIE Thank you. I'm not really a—

JOEL I know.

ARCHIE Just wanted to make sure. There was this one guy, I think he was from Cleveland, we got to my place, and he freaked out on me. I said to him, "You thought I was a *what?*" If he wasn't from Cleveland, he should have been.

JOEL People see what they want to see.

ARCHIE I can tell you what I see: red.

JOEL I'm Joel, by the way.

ARCHIE Roxie. My drag name is Roxie, my real name is Archie.

JOEL What would you like me to call you?

ARCHIE That's a good question. Archie—but thank you for asking. Do you smoke, Joel?

JOEL Not anymore.

ARCHIE Fuck. I mean, good for you, but fuck for me.

MARTIN (*offering him a cigarette*) Here.

ARCHIE You're being nice because you're scared of me.

MARTIN I'm not scared of you.

ARCHIE I don't want it.

MARTIN Come on.

ARCHIE I only smoke filter tips. Thanks anyway. (*to Joel*) No, when I look in the mirror, I see one ugly woman but one gorgeous drag queen. We owe Barbra so much. The courage to look ourselves. I think she's very beautiful. And don't say, "So are you." I'm beyond fishing. I hate to spend a fucking nickel in a fucking self-loathing place like this but I broke my fucking heel and I told my fucking girlfriend I'd meet her across the street. I feel like I'm on the Forbidden

Planet in here. No women, everybody's white—or should be! I feel like I died and went to hell. I will be so happy to take that A train with Carla to this drag party we're going to up on 138th Street. You could suffocate on the Shetland wool and musk oil in this place.

JOEL It's a present from my mother, every Christmas.

ARCHIE The musk oil or the sweater?

JOEL Both, actually.

ARCHIE Fuck, there I go, judging other people. Fuck me. If anybody should know better, it's a fucking drag queen from Bethpage, Long Island. I've been judged every fucking second of my fucking life. Why do we fucking do that to one another?

JOEL I think it's human nature.

ARCHIE Fuck human nature. God did not create us in His fucking image to fucking judge one another. Do you think I say "fuck" too much?

JOEL Fuck, no.

ARCHIE That was a joke, right?

JOEL Right.

ARCHIE We live in these little personal boxes and we break free only to find ourselves in a bigger box. I can break free for the rest of my life and still be in a box.

JOEL That sounds like a song cue.

ARCHIE How do you mean?

JOEL You're in a piano bar. We're all show queens.

ARCHIE Really? I can do that here?

He stands up from the bar.

ARCHIE (*cont.*) I would like to dedicate this number to every little boy or girl who grew up thinking they were meant to be somewhere else.

Archie sings a few bars of "Over the Rainbow."

ARCHIE (*cont.*) What are they yelling about across the street?

JOEL Their rights.

ARCHIE Good for them. There's Carla! (*waving*) I'm coming, sister. (*to Joel*) It sounds like they're having a good time out there. Come on, come with me.

JOEL Some other time.

ARCHIE Thank you. You're a kind man.

JOEL I'm just a frightened one sometimes.

ARCHIE No, you're kind. Believe me, I know from kind.

Archie starts to go.

ARCHIE (*cont.*) Fucking heels and fuck you, too, while I'm at it, fucking bartender. Fucking bars with fucking dress codes. (*He is gone.*)

TREY (*to Mary*) Do you know "Lonely Star" from *Summer Stock*?

MARY It's not a show tune. It's from a movie.

TREY Well excuse me!

JOEL You're crying.

ALEX So are you.

JOEL That song. Judy. Us.

ALEX What's wrong with us? Martin, *dos mas martinis, por favor!*

JOEL *Flores, flores para los muertos.*

ALEX I don't think they're the same thing.

JOEL On the way home, can we just look at what's happening out there?

ALEX I think we should.

JOEL Just look.

ALEX Absolutely. What's this from?

JOEL I don't know. It doesn't sound like anything. What's that from, Dennis?

PIANO MAN *Wish You Were Here.*

JOEL *Wish You Were Here?* There's no such show.

PIANO MAN 1952. The Imperial Theatre. Score by Harold Rome.

CLIFF I love, love, love the score for *Wish You Were Here.*

JOEL It's the beginning of the end, Alex. Gay Show Tune Senility. Our very own fatal disease.

ALEX I love you.

JOEL I know, Alex.

ALEX Would you marry me, if you could?

JOEL We are married.

ALEX You know what I mean.

JOEL   We're beyond that.

ALEX   I meant, if anything happens to me, what's going to happen to you?

JOEL   Nothing's going to happen to you.

ALEX   Honey, something happens to everyone at some point.

JOEL   We're not there yet and when we are, it'll be me first.

ALEX   You don't know that.

JOEL   You think I want to be around when you're not?

ALEX   I wasn't expecting that. I don't know what to say.

JOEL   Then don't say anything. It will do us both good.

He hugs Alex for a long time.

JOEL (*cont.*)   I'll be right back.

ALEX   Where are you going?

JOEL   It's a piano bar. I'm going to sing.

Joel sings with some of the men in the bar. Alex sings in counterpoint.

End of Act One

ACT TWO

Up in Harlem (1932)

Music. We are in a club in Harlem. It's a friendly place. The air is filled with bathtub gin and not a little marijuana smoke. The club is called Angel Eyes. MR. KEYS is at the piano. ANGEL EYES enters.

ANGEL EYES Welcome to Harlem. Welcome to Angel Eyes. Anybody here north of Seventy-second Street for the first time in their entire white Anglo-Saxon lives? I thought so. Come to experience the Harlem Renaissance for yourself. The booze and the dope and the dancing with your boyfriend got nothing to do with it. You're here for the culture. Am I right? You know I'm right. A white boy from Georgia told me he thought he'd died and gone to heaven when he came in here. The first person he met was Langston Hughes. He missed Zora Neale Hurston by five minutes, George Gershwin by ten. Is somebody on the door? I've been raided so many times this month, I think the police are beginning to like this place. My old friend Brick Top was in here the other night—she's got a club in Paris, very hoity-toity—and she said she taught the Prince of Wales to Charleston. I said to her, "Bricky, you bring the Prince of Wales to my place and we'll teach him to dance with a real hot black man, which you know His Highness is just itchin' to do. He ain't fooling nobody with that skinny Mrs. Simpson skaggy bitch of his."

To Mr. Keys, who is taking a big toke of weed.

ANGEL EYES (*cont.*) You think you can handle that?

MR. KEYS I feel like a Negro.

ANGEL EYES   That's funny, so do I. You ready, Mr. Keys?

MR. KEYS   I've been ready for sixteen bars.

The piano man is working on a song.

ANGEL EYES   I guess everybody knows this one.

He is officially into his act now.

ANGEL EYES (*cont.*)   The gentleman who wrote the words to it used to be a regular here. He was the one who named me Angel Eyes. I liked it. It stuck. I love the ladies, don't get me wrong, but why should they get all the compliments? Men like sweet talk, too. You know what I'm talking about? This one knows what I'm talking about!

Sings a stanza.

ANGEL EYES (*cont.*)   He was a short little guy, Jewish, kinda bald. He thought he was ugly. He drank too much. Maybe that's why.

Sings another stanza.

ANGEL EYES (*cont.*)   I remember his cufflinks. He was always playing with 'em. They were gold, of course. (*sings*) Everything was firstclass with him. Restaurants, the theatre, a box at the Polo Grounds. (*sings*) You know what he liked best? Me holding him in my arms and stroking his head until he fell asleep. Most bald men don't like their heads touched. Sometimes he would cry and couldn't stop. I mean, cry. I'd ask him why but he'd just shake his head, like he couldn't tell me, and cry some more.

Sings.

ANGEL EYES (*cont.*)   One time Mr.—one time my friend told me he was gonna write a song about me. "Sure you are," I said to him. I get that all the time. I'm gonna do this for ya, I'm gonna do that for ya. Never happens. Then one night we're lying there and I hear this woman on the radio singing "Ten Cents a Dance" and he says, "I wrote that. It's about you." And it was. You could have knocked me over with a feather. A guy like him keeping his word to a guy like me. Of course, you know me, I had to make some kind of a crack! "If it's about me, then why is some broad singing it?" and we both had a good laugh. That'll be the day— when a guy can sing a song like that about a guy like me.

Sings.

ANGEL EYES (*cont.*)   I heard he took up with a younger trick. That's what usually happens.

Sings.

ANGEL EYES (*cont.*)   Come on, big boy.

Transition.

AT THE BATHHOUSE (1975)

We are outside a bathhouse steam room. Men in towels are dimly seen. SCOOP and AARON are the first to appear through the mist.

AARON   Scoop! Did you see that, Scoop?

SCOOP   I saw it, Aaron.

AARON   I didn't know two men could do that. I'm a doctor and it's anatomically impossible. I bet it hurts, too.

SCOOP   Keep your voice down, Aaron.

AARON   This is the sort of thing that gives us a bad name.

SCOOP   You think everything gives us a bad name.

AARON   I hear them at the hospital, I hear what people are saying about gay men.

SCOOP   It's a sexual revolution and they're just jealous they're not a part of it.

AARON   So far tonight, neither are we.

He takes a hit of poppers.

SCOOP   Leave some for me.

He takes a hit of Aaron's poppers.

SCOOP (*cont.*)   From now on tonight, pretend we're not together. Act like you're alone.

AARON   You're the one who keeps talking to me.

Scoop disappears into the steam.

AARON (*cont.*)   Wait for me, Scoop!

Aaron disappears into the steam. More men in towels prowl about. Soon BRAD appears. He is followed by MENDY.

MENDY   Hi.

BRAD   Hi. It was getting a little intense in there. I like to see who's groping me.

MENDY   I was okay until those two old guys came back in. This place should have an age limit, like some of the bars do.

BRAD (*shrugging*)   They're okay as long as they just look.

MENDY   Yeah, but they all want to touch. What are you into?

BRAD   Just about everything.

MENDY You like to party?

BRAD I like to get high with the right guy.

MENDY I've got some Thai-stick and Quaaludes in my room.

BRAD Good stuff? There's a lot of shit going around.

MENDY Darling, this Thai-stick will have you coming for the next three weeks. Let's go. What's the matter?

BRAD I have a problem with men calling other men darling.

MENDY You do? Why?

BRAD I like men who are masculine.

MENDY So do I.

BRAD Fuck you.

MENDY You had your chance.

Starts away from Brad.

MENDY (*cont.*) Somebody thinks she's the Marlboro Man!

Next he goes to DARREN, who has come through the mists of steam.

MENDY (*cont.*) You don't mind if I call you "darling," do you?

DARREN I've been called a lot worse.

MENDY You want to do drugs and have wild sex with me?

DARREN Maybe later.

MENDY I may not be around later.

DARREN I'll take my chances.

Mendy goes. Brad goes up to Darren now.

BRAD Hi.

DARREN Hi.

BRAD You want to take this someplace else?

DARREN Sure, why not?

They disappear into the steam. Scoop and Aaron have seen them go off together.

AARON Let's go home, Scoop.

SCOOP You go home. We just got here.

AARON Fifteen more minutes, okay?

SCOOP This was your idea. "Let's go to the baths, Scoop, everyone else is!"

AARON I thought it would be fun.

SCOOP Just be yourself, Aaron.

AARON I am. It's not working.

Scoop goes back into the steam. Aaron remains as Bernie appears out of the steam.

AARON (*cont.*) Hi.

BERNIE Hi.

Carl appears out of the steam.

AARON Kind of a slow night tonight. Must be the weather.

BERNIE I wouldn't know. It's my first time here.

AARON You want to go to the show?

BERNIE What show?

AARON   In the nightclub at midnight. She's really good. The next big thing everybody's saying.

BERNIE   Maybe next time, excuse me.

He crosses to Carl.

BERNIE (*cont.*)   Hi.

CARL   Hi.

BERNIE   What's up?

CARL   Not much. You?

BERNIE   Not much. You looked like you might be leaving.

CARL   I was thinking about it. Not much happening.

BERNIE   I figured it was now or never. This is always the hard part, just saying hello. Hi.

CARL   Hi.

BERNIE   Hi.

CARL   Hi. Are you here with someone?

BERNIE   No.

CARL   I saw you talking to that guy.

BERNIE   No, he's just some guy.

Carl tweaks Bernie's nipples.

CARL   You like that?

BERNIE   Very much.

CARL   I think mine are wired to my dick. What else do you like?

BERNIE I'm not sure.

CARL You want to find out?

BERNIE I think I do.

CARL You got a room?

BERNIE It's on the third floor.

CARL I'm Carl.

BERNIE I'm Bernie.

CARL Hi.

BERNIE Hi.

They disappear in the steam. Aaron sees them go off together. A moment later and Scoop appears. He is with LESTER and JACKSON.

SCOOP Did you see that guy with the pierced nipples? Ouch, that must hurt.

JACKSON Usually there's a guy here with a Prince Albert.

SCOOP What's a Prince Albert?

JACKSON If you don't like pierced nipples, you don't want to know.

LESTER (*to Scoop*) Are you a top or a bottom? 'Cause I don't bottom for anyone, period, end of discussion.

JACKSON She bottoms.

LESTER That doesn't count. He was a movie star.

SCOOP Actually, I'm with him.

LESTER Bring him with you. Two's company, three's a crowd, but four's an orgy!

Lester and Jackson leave.

SCOOP You're right, Aaron, let's go home. This was a bad idea.

AARON If we hurry, we can still catch *Maude*.

Aaron and Scoop leave in the opposite direction as the lights come up on Bernie and Carl.

BERNIE You come here often?

CARL Looking for love in all the wrong places til the real thing comes along. What about you?

BERNIE It's my first time at the baths.

CARL They serve a purpose—just don't ask me what it is. I only wish they weren't such a firetrap.

BERNIE I worry about athlete's foot. Here we are. I asked for a room with a view but . . . ! At these prices, you'd expect a few amenities instead of a cubicle.

CARL I think we're the amenities and you are definitely the view. Where'd you get that scar?

BERNIE It looks worse than it was.

CARL Scars are sexy. (*He kisses it.*) What happened?

BERNIE Uncle Sam.

CARL You served?

BERNIE Korea. What about you?

CARL   I told the Army psychiatrist I was a homosexual. He told me I was suffering from "profound constitutional psycho-pathetic inferiority." I told him I'd rather be a homosexual. I was 4-F like that.

BERNIE   You had more guts than I did.

CARL   I figure it's their loss.

Carl starts to take off Bernie's towel.

BERNIE   What are you doing? I'm a little over my ideal weight. Breyer's came out with a new flavor last month: Vanilla Cherry Swirl. Have you tried it?

CARL   No.

BERNIE   Don't. It's addictive. They should make anything that good illegal. So tell me about yourself. What do you do?

CARL   I'm a high school librarian.

BERNIE   Really?

CARL   I know, it's very gay.

BERNIE   I'm in advertising, which is gayer. You have nothing on me. What?

They look at each other and like more and more what they see.

CARL   Listen, there's something about me you should know up front.

BERNIE   Here it comes.

CARL   I live on Staten Island.

BERNIE So did Walt Whitman. I thought you were gonna tell me you had a lover. I live on West Seventy-fourth Street.

Short pause. They look at each other.

CARL Now it's my turn, what?

BERNIE I'm feeling sort of overwhelmed right now.

CARL Me, too. I didn't expect this.

BERNIE Neither did I.

CARL You wanna get married?

BERNIE I'm old-fashioned. I think we should have a second date first.

CARL I'm still waiting for you to tell me you've got a lover and you only do this when he's out of town.

BERNIE Is that what you were thinking?

CARL Why wouldn't you? You're a terrific-looking guy, you've got a smile that could break a heart and you know who Walt Whitman is.

BERNIE I was married to a woman. We had a couple of kids.

CARL Okay.

BERNIE It was a bad divorce. My kids don't want to see me.

CARL That must be rough.

BERNIE It is.

CARL If you ever want to talk about it—I think I'm a pretty good listener.

BERNIE It's a long story.

CARL I'd like to hear it.

BERNIE I don't come off so good in it.

CARL Why don't you let me be the judge of that?

Bernie kisses Carl's nipples.

BERNIE You like that?

CARL I'm Sicilian. I like everything.

He takes Bernie's face in his hands.

BERNIE I just started doing this.

CARL Bernie.

BERNIE I like it when you say my name.

CARL It's going to be all right, Bernie.

BERNIE What is?

CARL Everything.

They have begun to make love. Transition.

A Hospital (1989)

The visitor's lounge. It's noisy and crowded. People are having a good time. They have forgotten, if only for a moment, where they are and what they are doing there. One of them, SEB, *is wearing an Act Up T-shirt.*

NURSE JACK So I said to him, "Honey, I don't care who you were in *A Chorus Line* or how cute you were, 'cause you're not in *A Chorus Line* now and you're not looking so hot either."

RICHARD   He didn't even create the role. He was like the nine hundred and fiftieth replacement.

NURSE JACK   The fifth floor has ways of dealing with Queens of Attitude.

RICHARD   Our very own Nurse Ratchet!

SEB   Do you think you men could show a little respect and compassion for your brothers who are dying?

RICHARD   Lighten up, Seb.

SEB   What if that was Gary he was talking about, Richard?

RICHARD   Gary is going to get well.

SEB   Most of these men aren't!

RICHARD   Gary isn't dying.

BERNIE   Everybody calm down.

SEB   I don't think AIDS is funny.

NURSE JACK   Everyone in this hospital is doing their best, mister. You got any suggestions for us, take them to Sister Margaret in Administration. She eats people like you for breakfast.

Aaron comes into the waiting area.

AARON   What's going on here? I could hear you from the nurses' station.

NURSE JACK   Nerves are getting a little frayed, Doctor, that's all.

AARON   The last I heard, St. Vincent's was still a serious hospital, not *The Tonight Show.*

RICHARD We'll keep it down, Doctor.

AARON How is he today, Richard?

RICHARD Good. Better, I think.

AARON We're going to have to put those lead shields inside his eyelids again, I'm afraid.

RICHARD They just took them out!

AARON I'm sorry, but this new protocol requires them.

RICHARD He's not going to like that.

AARON You want to tell him or should I?

RICHARD No way I'm going to.

AARON That's why they pay me the big bucks.

RICHARD Thanks, Aaron.

AARON (*to Spencer*) You're a new face.

SPENCER I'm Gary's brother, Spencer.

AARON His brother? How many brothers do you have?

SPENCER Just Gary. I couldn't get away before this.

AARON Something more pressing?

SPENCER Of course not. It's my busiest time of year.

AARON Where's your partner?

SPENCER My wife's in L.A. with the kids. I'm not gay.

AARON That wasn't my question. (*to Seb*) Where's your pass, young man?

SEB Give me a break, Doctor.

AARON You can visit during open visiting hours like everyone else.

SEB That asshole gets to visit Gary just because he's his brother? I'm his best friend.

RICHARD Chill, Seb.

SEB You chill, Richard.

AARON Keep your voice down or I'll have you taken out and you won't ever get back up to this floor.

SEB Who's gonna stop me? That bull dyke head nurse by the elevator?

AARON That bull dyke works eighteen-hour shifts and asked to be on this floor. Sometimes I wonder if AIDS had happened to the lesbian community what our response would have been and sometimes I think I don't want to know the answer. Next time, get a pass.

SEB Yes, sir.

AARON And thank that bull dyke on your way out.

He goes.

RICHARD That is one terrific doctor, even if he is a ballbreaker.

BERNIE You think he's gay, Richard?

RICHARD I don't care what anyone is anymore, Bernie, I just want to take Gary home.

BERNIE You want to get some rest? I'll cover for you.

RICHARD I'm fine, but isn't Carl back yet?

BERNIE Tomorrow. I'm bachelor-at-large for another twenty-four hours. Why the National Association of High School Librarians has to have their annual powwow in Chicago this time of year!

RICHARD What do librarians talk about for a week?

BERNIE The Dewey Decimal system.

RICHARD And that's when the high jinks begin! Give him our love.

SPENCER I'm sorry I couldn't come before this, Richard.

RICHARD Gary was too, Spencer.

Piano Man has been sitting apart from the others.

BERNIE Who's that?

RICHARD He plays the piano. He's been around town for years. His partner was just admitted.

BERNIE Jesus Christ, this thing!

RICHARD I think he's sort of hot.

BERNIE You're incorrigible.

RICHARD So was Gary. That's why we were a good team. I said "was." I mean "is." So is Gary. That's why we are a good team.

GARY *comes out of his room.*

GARY I'm cured. The doctor says we can go to Fantasy Fest in Key West and make it back in time for the Halloween Parade. This year, I think I'll go as Ann-Margret in *Viva Las Vegas.* That's known as gay humor, little brother.

RICHARD Will you marry me?

GARY We're beyond marriage.

RICHARD I'm serious. If I ask Father Tom when he makes his rounds, will you marry me?

NURSE JACK That's a great idea.

GARY You keep out of this.

RICHARD Father Tom's cool. I bet he will.

GARY He's also Catholic. I bet he won't.

SEB He's also gay. I'll out him if he doesn't.

RICHARD I'm serious. Will you marry me, Gary what-was-your-last-name again?

GARY I don't want to get married. I want to get well.

RICHARD Did I ever tell you guys how we met?

GARY Only about a million times, Richard.

RICHARD It was at a demonstration on the Mall in D.C. I went to Washington and marched for gay rights and I got zilch. Two years later, I go to Washington with my best friend Ellen to march for pro-choice and I get Gary.

As RICHARD *speaks, his words are more and more just for Gary. The others, sensing it's time to leave the two men alone, will move out of the area.*

BERNIE Where *is* Ellen?

SEB Seattle, her mother's sick. Anybody want anything from the cafeteria?

SPENCER May I come with you?

SEB Sure.

SPENCER *and Seb go. Richard is holding Gary.*

RICHARD I said to her, "See that guy in the white T-shirt yelling 'U.S. out of my uterus'?" And she said, "Richard, I think everyone in Washington, D.C., sees that guy in the white T-shirt yelling 'U.S. out of my uterus'!" Then I said, "He doesn't know it but I'm going to marry him. If he doesn't live in Brooklyn, I'm going to spend the rest of my life with him." And I did. Didn't I, babe, didn't I?

GARY Only you, Richard, would fall in love with a guy yelling "U.S. out of my uterus"!

RICHARD What's the matter?

GARY I don't feel so good.

NURSE JACK, *Richard and Gary go back into Gary's room. Only Bernie and the Piano Man remain.*

BERNIE Old friends. We get a little boisterous. Sorry.

PIANO MAN It beats the other stuff.

BERNIE How is your partner doing today? He's Allen, right?

PIANO MAN Better, thank you. Yes, Allen. A little better, they said.

BERNIE Good. That's good. How long have you been together?

PIANO MAN Only six weeks but if I have anything to say about it, it's going to be for a long time. You?

BERNIE Carl and I have been together for fourteen years now.

PIANO MAN Wow!

BERNIE I know.

PIANO MAN I knew he was positive when I met him. I didn't care. I still don't. I love him.

BERNIE Good luck.

PIANO MAN Thanks.

Bernie goes. Piano Man sits a moment and then goes to piano and plays. Transition.

A LONG-TERM RELATIONSHIP (1998)

Washington Square Park. A warm summer day. We hear children playing, off. Fritz and Pat are interviewing Scoop and Aaron. Pat has a recording device.

AARON I met Scoop my senior year at Tufts. He was studying for a career in the Foreign Service. I was pre-med. We were both wearing tie-dyed T-shirts and bell-bottoms.

SCOOP They don't want to hear this sort of stuff, Aaron.

FRITZ We do, we do. Don't we?

PAT Don't stop, I'm taping.

AARON It was at a Bob Dylan concert. I thought he was incredibly sexy.

SCOOP I thought you were, too.

AARON I was talking about Dylan. I stopped feeding this one's ego years ago. You have heard of Bob Dylan?

FRITZ Oh, sure. There's a seminar on him at school.

AARON I had such a crush on him.

PAT Our professor thinks he was queer.

AARON What do you mean was? He's very much still with us and I've never heard anyone even suggest he was gay.

PAT Professor Hollings thinks an argument can be made that anyone who is countercultural is queer.

FRITZ Why? You have a problem with Dylan being queer?

AARON Yes. I have a problem with anyone being called queer who isn't.

FRITZ That's called internalized homophobia.

AARON No, it's called inaccuracy.

SCOOP What is this interview for again?

PAT We're gender studies majors at Vassar. Our professor said we should talk to some elder queers and find out what it was like to be part of the pre-Stonewall oppressed and non-liberated generation.

SCOOP And we fit the bill?

FRITZ Exactly! As a queer theorist, I find the oral history of an elder queer in his fifties or sixties—or late forties even!— is worth more than a whole library full of sociological studies. Who else is going to tell us who we were or where we've been better than guys like you?

AARON Thank you . . . ?

FRITZ Fritz. And this is my friend, Pat.

AARON Pat! I was wondering. It's a good name for gender studies.

PAT Men like you are the keepers of the flame. Our very own Dead Sea Scrolls. You lived through the years of secrecy and oppression that would have decimated a lesser people.

AARON Now we're a people. I thought we were just old queers.

PAT I don't mean it to be offensive. I'm a young queer. We're becoming a people.

AARON That doesn't work for me. Blacks are a people, Jews are a people.

SCOOP Gays are a people, honey—people who need people.

AARON I'm sorry but we have a lot of trouble with that word, queer.

FRITZ Get used to it. It isn't going away. If we reclaim it, no one can hurt us with it anymore. Besides, it's easier than GBLTTIQ.

AARON GBLTT-*what?*

FRITZ Gay-Bisexual-Lesbian-Transgender-Two Spirit-Intersex Questioning. Now where were we?

AARON A Bob Dylan concert. It was love at first sight.

SCOOP You got that part right. It's not that we weren't gay before we met; it's more like we weren't really anything.

AARON I thought I was in love with a woman, but not in the way I was soon in love with Scoop. His real name isn't Scoop, by the way.

SCOOP They know that. Nobody's real name is Scoop. It's Alice.

PAT But neither of you was really out?

AARON That was a joke.

PAT I got that.

AARON But you chose not to laugh.

PAT I didn't think it was funny. Gay humor has come a long way since the days when we could refer to one another as "Alice" or "Mary" and get a laugh.

AARON We've come a long way, baby.

SCOOP Aaron and I were out to one another.

PAT But we have to be out to the entire world. I can't imagine living your life not being out to everyone.

FRITZ What happened to you and the Foreign Service?

SCOOP It was made pretty clear to me that as a gay man the best I could expect was a menial posting in some remote corner of the globe. Too remote and too menial for me anyway. Goodbye Foreign Service, hello landscaping.

AARON I hate to break it to you but we did okay for ourselves.

FRITZ You were oppressed by the straight white male patriarchy.

AARON We were?

SCOOP When you put it like that, it sounds terrific.

AARON Our lives were figuring out how to be happy despite the obstacles. That's what we really were in those days: great gay improvisers.

PAT How gay was it in those days?

AARON It was pretty gay. Gay enough for me anyway.

SCOOP People called themselves Bohemians but we knew better. We had our codes for knowing one another: colored bandanas in our back pocket. Red on your left side meant one thing. Grey on your right meant something else.

AARON If you weren't careful you ended up going home with some guy who thought you wanted him to set you on fire and then pee on you to put it out.

SCOOP That was me, Aaron. He loved it. We had hard-to-find bars down dark little side streets with backrooms where we could dance.

AARON What was the name of that place on West Tenth St? You had to go down all those stairs? It was a real firetrap. Lenny's! It was called Lenny's Hideaway! We saw Rock Hudson there once.

FRITZ Another victim of the closet.

AARON Be that as it may, he left with the best-looking guy there.

SCOOP Remember the San Remo on Bleecker Street? You'd see Allen Ginsberg, Leonard Bernstein, James Baldwin sometimes, but it wasn't a quote gay bar. You went there to talk. You drank, you smoked, you gaped at your idols. I saw Samuel Beckett there, the one and only time he was ever in New York. He wasn't gay but *Samuel Beckett!* It was wonderful.

AARON I think it's a Starbuck's now.

FRITZ Everyone knows the Village is dead now.

AARON It is?

FRITZ Look around you, nothing but bourgeois baby boomers. They want eighteen hundred for a fourth-floor studio walk-up.

PAT Let's stay on point, Fritz. Who were your role models? People like Benjamin Britten and Peter Pears? W.H. Auden and Chester Kallman?

SCOOP No, people like Zachary.

AARON He wrote *the* book on Milton.

SCOOP People like Joel and Alex.

AARON Those two and their show tunes!

PAT Who were they?

AARON Friends who fought the good fight.

PAT Would they talk to us?

SCOOP You're a little late.

PAT I'm sorry.

AARON We had a gay dentist.

SCOOP We did? And I let him put his hands in my mouth?

AARON Oh, sure. We were always pushing the envelope. We ate at gay restaurants. We owned property on Fire Island. We produced and starred in the Cherry Grove Follies for three record-breaking summers. We had certain public places we felt pretty safe: the Rambles in Central Park; the Meat Rack on the west side of Washington Square Park. The piers! Not that either of us ever frequented any of those places.

SCOOP I loved standing room at the Old Met. You got good music and a hand job at the same time. Of course, you had to know when. I remember once during the second act of *Tosca* hearing this really loud voice: "I told you, mister, not during *Vissi d'Arte*." The whole audience heard it. I swear, even Maria Callas stopped singing.

AARON I loved the baths. God, that was a time! Bette Midler was ours and ours alone.

SCOOP Aaron thinks he discovered her.

AARON I did. Ask her!

SCOOP And then nine men died at the Everhard Baths for no reason except the owners didn't think they deserved the same fire exits as everyone else.

AARON Nine men but it felt like nine hundred.

PAT What else do you miss?

SCOOP I had such a thing for Casey Donovan. He was my ultimate sexual fantasy, present company excluded.

AARON He was everybody's fantasy. Those legs, that smile, that dick. You probably don't know who we're talking about.

PAT Oh, sure. We had a Casey Donovan film retrospective at school last semester. We showed *Boys in the Sand, The Back Row,* a couple of others.

AARON I haven't seen one in years. How do they hold up?

PAT It's pretty unsettling to watch all those men having unprotected sex.

FRITZ You guys were so wild. I mean, wow!

SCOOP When he died, I remember thinking, it's over, it's all over.

PAT What was?

SCOOP The party.

PAT You're talking about AIDS now?

SCOOP No, I'm talking about the party. We were the princes of New York, weren't we, honey?

AARON Some kind of royalty! There was our New York and then there was everybody else's. (*to Pat and Fritz*) We could go on like this.

SCOOP Is this the sort of stuff you want?

FRITZ Are you telling me it was better then?

SCOOP It was different then. We didn't make so much of a fuss. Maybe we should have. I appreciate your professor and I love what you're trying to do but we can't rewrite our history to suit you.

AARON I thought it was rather a Golden Age myself but that's just my opinion.

SCOOP Silver, anyway.

FRITZ Are you telling us we fought the police at Stonewall and petitioned the legislatures for change when we didn't have to? That we screamed our guts out so fewer men would die from AIDS but we shouldn't have bothered?

SCOOP We're very glad you did.

FRITZ Gay men and lesbians are no longer willing or able to stay in the closet of repression and hypocrisy that your generation lived in all your lives, and you're saying it wasn't so bad in there after all!

SCOOP I guess it was bad. We didn't know we could change it. We just wanted to be happy.

AARON And despite everything your generation might think, we were. Some people would admire us.

FRITZ I'm afraid I'm not one of them. Thanks for your time anyway.

PAT Self-loathing can run so deep.

FRITZ What about those two lesbians by the fountain? They look cool. Professor Hollings is going to want gender parity in our report.

Fritz and Pat leave.

AARON They were fun. What's the matter?

SCOOP We're a couple of non-threatening, assimilated homosexuals. We're out, we're proud and nobody notices. It pisses me off.

AARON You, not me.

SCOOP No, really, I see those men in feathers and heels at the Pride Parade and wonder if we've missed some essential part of the Gay Experience? Or those guys in leather and chains on their Harleys. Are they in touch with something we're not?

AARON You want a good flogging, darling? I'll give you one.

SCOOP Not tonight, honey, I have a headache.

AARON I came home from work at St. Vincent's a couple of weeks ago and I stood in the door watching you asleep in your chair with Charlie in your lap and I thought how blessed I was to have this man and this dog in my life.

SCOOP I feel the same way.

AARON Let me finish. I also thought, what a waste. My partner could have been the Ambassador to the Court of St. James but instead he owns a landscaping business and volunteers three days a week at the AIDS hospice.

SCOOP I'm happy.

AARON I know but are you all you might have been?

SCOOP I'm with you, that's everything I want to be.

AARON Did you give up the life you wanted and deserved because of me?

SCOOP No, a thousand times no.

AARON If I'd been a woman, I'd have married you and been your wife and had your children.

SCOOP If you'd been a woman, maybe you wouldn't have been a doctor. Everybody's come a long way. We're all winners.

They hug.

SCOOP *(cont.)* The Cherry Grove Follies! Those were the days.

AARON We were sensational.

They begin to sing and dance their "big" number: "Run Rabbit Run" by Noel Gay. They stop when they hear familiar bells.

SCOOP There's the ice cream man. Do we dare?

AARON That's another long-term relationship perk we should have told them about.

SCOOP What?

AARON We said goodbye to our waistlines years ago.

Scoop and Aaron go. Transition.

SUR LA MER II (2005)

A stretch of beach. We hear the ocean. Gulls fly above. MARCUS and PERRY are barefoot and their trousers are rolled up. There is a beach blanket with a picnic hamper nearby. Bernie and Carl have laid out a very nice spread and are enjoying it. They are looking and pointing at a house in the dunes which we cannot see. Perry has a copy of a glossy architectural magazine with him.

PERRY Listen to this, Marcus: "*Sur La Mer*, the Goldmans' 'summer cottage' had eight bedrooms, all *en suite,* plus a great room, a library, a billiards room, a ballroom and two dining rooms, family and formal."

MARCUS To think people actually lived like that!

PERRY What do you mean, lived? They still do.

MARCUS Yeah, rich bastards.

PERRY The Goldmans had something better than money— they had help.

MARCUS Don't look at me when you say that!

PERRY I wonder which one of those windows was Padraic's room?

MARCUS Over the garage, probably. That's where we're going to put our chauffeur.

PERRY I bet they did it right here on the beach. Made love under the stars and then skinny-dipped in the Atlantic.

MARCUS I doubt it, Perry.

PERRY Why?

MARCUS Jews are afraid of the ocean. They just wade.

BERNIE Where's the salt, Carl?

CARL Right in front of you, Bernie. Are you wearing your sun block?

BERNIE It's not that kind of sun.

CARL You heard the doctor: moisturize, moisturize, moisturize.

BERNIE Aren't you going to eat that?

Perry has seen people approaching along the beach.

PERRY Gay dad alert.

CARL You can tell from this distance?

PERRY Oh sure, absolutely.

CARL Sometimes I think everybody's gay, Perry, even your father!

PERRY Dad, were you ever actually inside Sur la Mer?

BERNIE A couple of times as a kid—and we looked in all the windows once, one off-season.

PERRY You and Carl?

CARL   No, he was with one of his other boyfriends.

BERNIE   I was with your mother. It was before you were born. She was pregnant with you.

MARCUS   Thirty-four long years ago next month!

PERRY   Ha ha ha!

CARL   Isn't it wonderful to have an old boyfriend, Marcus?

MARCUS   Perry's too old to call him my boyfriend.

CARL   I call Bernie my boyfriend.

MARCUS   That's sort of my point, Carl.

BERNIE   Don't get him started!

MARCUS   Perry's my spouse.

BERNIE   (*low*)   Not in this state, he isn't, Marcus.

MARCUS   So what happened to the Jewish banker and his Irish chauffeur who were too hot not to cool down?

BERNIE   Eventually, they both got married and had families, but they never stopped seeing one another. When David Goldman died, he left my grandfather Padraic twenty-five thousand dollars, which he in turn left to my father, which is how he got his start in business.

PERRY   I am the love child of a Jewish banker and a probably illiterate Irish chauffeur who didn't even have the key to the front door of his lover's house.

MARCUS   Now I know where Perry gets his uniform fetish from.

PERRY   I do not have a uniform fetish.

MARCUS Every time we see a guy in a uniform—a cop, a sailor, even a FedEx—his gaze wanders.

PERRY You're not supposed to notice.

MARCUS I'm your partner, I notice everything.

BERNIE That word I can live with.

CARL Bernie?

BERNIE What?

CARL Nobody asked you.

MARCUS I'm glad we did this. It's important—it's our history. My own gay roots aren't so la-te-da. My mother's cousin had a gay club in Harlem. Family legend is he taught the King of England to Charleston.

PERRY We should try to find it.

Cell phone rings.

MARCUS It's her.

PERRY Who else?

Marcus answers.

MARCUS Hello? Hi, how are you? We're at the beach. East Hampton. It's about a hundred miles from the city. No, rich people have places here. We're not rich.

BERNIE Who is it?

PERRY The birth mom.

BERNIE So you're really going through with this?

CARL Bernie!

PERRY   We told you we were.

BERNIE   I hope you know what you're getting into.

PERRY   Don't start, Dad.

MARCUS   Well, no washer/dryer lasts forever, Monica.

PERRY   What does she want this time?

MARCUS   How much is a new one?

PERRY   Where does it stop with that woman?

MARCUS   Charge it and send us the bill. And tell the doctor to send us your drug tests. Of course we trust you. It's just that we need all this documentation for when everything is final . . . How is the baby, Monica? . . . You said "she." You distinctly said "she." I told you: We didn't want to know. We *all* slip, Monica, only some slips are a little more serious than others . . . I'm sorry, go watch your football game. He sounds like a nice guy. I'm glad you're happy. Perry and I are happy, too.

Ends call.

MARCUS (*cont.*)   She hung up before I could say that.

PERRY   My dad's worried we're not going to make good fathers.

CARL   He's worried you guys haven't thought this baby thing through, Marcus, that's all.

Two attractive men come along the beach. They are carrying an infant in a blanket. They are MEL and DICK.

PERRY   Hello.

MEL   Hi.

DICK   Hi.

General hellos and looking at the baby.

MEL   Do you believe this weather? September is the best time of year out here.

DICK   We've been out all week. It's been Hampton Heaven Bliss.

MEL   No more dreaded Summer People, hurrah!

PERRY (*to the infant*)   Hello, little angel. (*to Mel and Dick*) What's her name? She's a doll.

DICK   Tristan, he's a boy.

MARCUS   I love his outfit. Where did you get it?

MEL   Chelsea Baby on Eighth Avenue.

MARCUS   I should have guessed. They've got great stuff.

PERRY   We're adopting. The mother's due in eight weeks.

DICK   Welcome to the club. Boy or girl?

MARCUS   A girl. We just found out. We told the mother we didn't want to know but she was high on crystal meth or something.

PERRY   Marcus! He's kidding.

DICK   Girls are great, too.

MEL   I think a girl would have scared us. With a boy all you have to do is learn how to throw a ball . . . (*he sings*) . . . "but you gotta be a father to a girl!"

DICK We have very modest goals for this little fella: an Oscar, a couple of Wimbledon titles and the Nobel Prize for curing cancer.

MEL I'll settle for healthy, happy and the love of a good man.

DICK Or woman. We're not going to raise him gay. Whatever *that* means!

BERNIE I think I have a pretty good idea.

CARL Stop it, Bernie.

MARCUS Was it an open adoption?

DICK His mother is Latina and lives in Guatemala. Where's your birth mom?

MARCUS She's in Pittsburgh with her dealer boyfriend.

PERRY She is not! We're working with a great lawyer.

DICK You need a great lawyer.

MEL Ours was great and cute. Derek Jeter in Armani. I nearly left this one for him.

DICK I bet you're getting cold feet right about now? We sure did.

MARCUS Only a little.

MEL Don't worry. It turned out to be the best thing we ever did. Babies put everything into perspective. They're very humbling and very, I don't know, *enlarging* at the same time. I used to think we were the only two people on this planet. Well, Georgica Beach anyway.

DICK Of course you gotta learn to love changing diapers. Where's your place out here?

PERRY No, we're just out from the city for the day with my father and his partner.

BERNIE We're dreaded non-residents. Hi. I'm Bernie, Perry's dad.

CARL Carl! Hello.

MEL Your dad and his boyfriend? That is so cool. I'm Mel, this is my husband, Richard or Dick, also known as Spider!

PERRY What do you call him?

MEL All three! And you're . . . ?

PERRY Perry and this is my husband, Marcus.

BERNIE (*low, to Carl*) Jesus!

MARCUS Finally, he's making an honest man out of me. You've never called me that before.

DICK We're registered as domestic partners in New York, had a civil union in Vermont and we got married in Toronto and Boston.

MEL We covered all our bases. You sort of have to with a kid.

MARCUS Perry and I are registered as domestic partners.

DICK What about you two?

CARL We're still living in sin.

DICK Would you guys like to have a drink? We're right up there.

PERRY That's your place? Sur La Mer is yours?

MEL I told Richard we're going to have to sell it if we want to get this one into a good kindergarten.

PERRY We've got some ancient family history with that house. My great-grandfather worked for the people who owned it.

MARCUS That's putting it mildly. He was the owner's lover. That was their love nest.

DICK Sounds like good dish to me. You can tell us over Cosmos. You'll come?

MARCUS Thanks.

PERRY Just let us get our stuff. We'll be right up.

MEL Somebody needs changing.

DICK He's drooling, Mel. When did you burp him last?

MEL About five minutes ago.

DICK That's not enough. The book said every two or three.

They head off toward Sur la Mer.

PERRY Do you see my sunglasses, honey?

BERNIE We're not going up there, are we?

PERRY Why not?

BERNIE Men like that are disgusting. My husband! Tristan! Babies are not accessories you buy from impoverished Third World women. Babies are people; the women who bear them are people.

CARL You're on a soapbox, Bernie.

BERNIE   What kind of life are they going to provide for that child?

PERRY   A better one than he would have gotten in a shack with a mud floor and no water or electricity. I didn't know you were so against us adopting this child.

BERNIE   What if you two break up?

MARCUS   We're not going to break up, Bernie.

BERNIE   He broke up with Edward, Marcus.

PERRY   Edward was an asshole.

BERNIE   They bought an apartment together.

MARCUS   We're not going to break up, Bernie.

PERRY   Dad, would you have said that to a straight couple? "Congratulations on the baby. Now when are you two going to get a divorce?" Coming from you, I find that remark especially offensive.

CARL   Everybody calm down.

PERRY   Our child will know and love us as out and proud parents. What did my sister and I and our mom know you as?

CARL   You're out of line, Perry.

PERRY   He got married, had kids and then came out. That's the way they did things. Very traditional, very fucked up. Marcus and I aren't going to inflict that kind of trauma on our kids.

BERNIE   How can you be sure of that?

PERRY We're not sure of anything. We'll make mistakes but they won't be your mistakes. You were a great role model in that department. You said you were proud of me when I came out to you. Why does it stop there? Why doesn't it include the rest of me? Did you find my sunglasses, honey?

CARL I'm sure you'll make wonderful parents.

MARCUS Don't patronize us, Carl.

PERRY A little support would be appreciated.

MARCUS Let's go visit your ancestral home, honey.

They start off toward the house. Bernie calls after Perry.

BERNIE We'll talk, Perry! (*then, to Carl*) Coming here was a terrible idea.

CARL Sur La Mer's not why you're fighting.

BERNIE I don't think they're ready for this.

CARL That's not your call, Bernie.

BERNIE Wasn't it enough I worried he'd get AIDS all these years?

CARL Of course you did. He's your son.

BERNIE I was so happy when he met Marcus and settled down.

CARL Me, too.

BERNIE You're lucky you're not a parent.

CARL That's funny, I was thinking you're lucky you are. Come on, they're waiting for us.

BERNIE   You're going up there?

CARL   And I think you should, too.

Carl leaves Bernie standing there. He looks in the direction the others have taken.

BERNIE   I'm sorry. I'm sorry!

He realizes they can't hear him over the sound of the ocean. He takes a deep breath and starts off in the direction the others took. Transition.

THE GROUP

Six men are sitting in a circle. One of them, Pat, is wearing a Vassar sweatshirt. GORDON is standing behind them, facilitating.

LEWIS   And then he said, "Son, I will never be ashamed of you." I just broke down and cried when he said that. I actually put my head in his lap and wept. I thought I knew my own father and I didn't know him at all. I thought he was just this rough, tough guy who didn't even like me. He told me he loved me.

LEWIS's story is received with much approval.

LEWIS (*cont.*)   Thanks, guys. Oh, PS, we got the condo in P-town over the Fourth again—the one we had last summer and thought we'd lost. Tim is so happy.

GORDON   That's great, Lewis. Who wants to go next?

MARTY   I don't think I'm going to be in group in September. I feel I've gotten everything out of it I can and I don't feel I have much more to contribute.

LEWIS   You have a lot to contribute, Marty.

MARTY Thank you, Lewis. I just feel I'm on empty right now. I need to . . . I don't know . . . just not be here for a while.

LEWIS I for one will miss you and I hope you change your mind.

PAT Me, too, Marty.

MARTY Thank you. Anyway, I promised myself I'd sit down and finally write that book about my Uncle Archie I told you about.

PAT The drag queen? That is so important. We need stories like hers.

MARTY I'm gonna try. That's wonderful about you and your father, Lewis.

LEWIS Good luck with yours.

MARTY I need more than luck with that son of a bitch.

GORDON Who else?

PAT If nobody's doing anything, Queers For A Moral Universe are meeting at the center Sunday afternoon.

MICHAEL You can take the girl out of Vassar but you can't take Vassar out of the girl.

GORDON Hey!

JOSEPH We're going to have to put Ginger Rogers down.

LEWIS What did the vet say?

JOSEPH There's nothing they can do.

PAT How many years have you had her?

JOSEPH It feels like forever. It's six years since Danny passed. We got her at least five years before that.

MICHAEL We had a cat that lived almost fifteen years.

LEWIS Are you gonna get another one?

JOSEPH I haven't thought about that. She's not dead yet.

LEWIS I'm sorry. That was inappropriate.

JOSEPH It wasn't inappropriate, just insensitive. No wonder you have a new boyfriend every six weeks.

LEWIS I don't have a new boyfriend every six weeks.

JOSEPH Some of us have feelings that last a little longer than thirty seconds.

LEWIS If you want to choose to mourn Danny for the rest of your life and be one of those full-time widows, that's your decision. But that's all it is: a decision. Some of us move on. That's our choice. It doesn't mean we feel any less deeply or passionately than you. And if you're talking about me and Roger, that was sex, pure sex. Does anyone have a problem with that? That's what gay men do: sleep with other gay men. If I wanted to get married, I would. I certainly wouldn't be in group talking about it.

MARTY (*He does a pretty good Bette Davis.*) "But you are, Blanche, but you are!"

GORDON Marty!

MARTY I'm sorry.

GORDON You know better than that.

MARTY I'm sorry, sorry, sorry.

GORDON Who else? This is our last group until after Labor Day, gentlemen. Michael?

MICHAEL This is hard.

JOSEPH Were you trolling the Internet again, Michael?

Reaction from others.

PAT I know someone so dumb he used his own name in the chat rooms.

JOSEPH Some of the names people come up with for themselves—Top Dog!

LEWIS I wouldn't be surprised if one of these days we all wound up in the same chat room and I spend an hour trying to pick you up, Marty.

MARTY I don't have a computer.

JOSEPH You don't have a life.

GORDON I believe Michael has the floor.

MICHAEL I picked a guy up the other night.

Reactions from group.

JOSEPH I hope his name was Eugene. You're getting married next month, Michael.

MICHAEL Do you want to hear this or don't you? We were in an elevator. He said hi. Right off I saw he was wearing a wedding band. We had a drink. He said he was married and straight but fooled around. I'm sure he was a member in good standing of the Moral Majority. Straight men who have sex with us usually are.

MARTY And they always say it's their first time.

GORDON Marty!

KURT And they're usually drunk, right-wing religious nutbags.

MICHAEL I didn't want to know who he'd voted for.

GORDON You men are out of control tonight.

MICHAEL Anyway, we went to his apartment. He said his wife was out of town. Eugene was, too. Actually, he's still on the West Coast working on that Susan Sarandon/Tim Robbins project, but I would never bring someone back to our place. I did once and it freaked me out. It was our home and I'd made it a fuck pad. Never again, I swore.

PAT I love Susan Sarandon and Tim Robbins.

LEWIS Can we cut to the chase? We've only got a few more minutes.

MICHAEL He asked me to tie him up and fuck him.

Reactions from the group.

MARTY I'm taking back my wedding present.

MICHAEL I said okay.

JOSEPH When do you ever say "no," Michael?

MICHAEL It's not my scene but he was very attractive and we smoked a joint.

Negative reaction from the group.

MARTY Betty Ford will have something to say about that.

MICHAEL It's the first one I've had since New Year's Eve.

LEWIS Jesus, Michael!

MICHAEL   He goes into the closet and he's got all this bondage gear hidden away in his gym bag and to make a long story short, I've got him tied up and then he says he has to be gagged first, too, and so I gag him and he does look kinda sexy still and I'm hard, so I fuck him but fast and without much feeling and when I pull out I suddenly feel such a revulsion for him and what I've done that I want to do something really awful to him. I told him that, too. I said "I want to do something terrible to you" and he just nodded and shook his head, like that is exactly what he wanted me to do. You know what I did? This is what I did. I took his ring.

He has the ring in his hand.

MICHAEL (*cont.*)   What is marriage? What does this ring mean? Does this mean he loves her? Can you love someone and wear a ring and still ask a stranger to come home with you and tie you up and fuck you?

He puts the wedding band on his left fourth finger.

MICHAEL (*cont.*)   Will a ring mean I love Eugene when we get married next month? Does marriage mean we don't sleep with other people? I can't stop or maybe I don't want to, which? I want to be faithful to my partner and I can't be.

Sliding the ring on and off his finger.

MICHAEL (*cont.*)   Michael and Eugene, Eugene and Michael.

Then.

MICHAEL (*cont.*)   I left him there like that, trussed up like a turkey, and told the doorman that Mr. Martin in 14D needed his help ASAP.

GORDON   Any comments?

JOSEPH That's a fine note to end group on.

GORDON That's a judgment, Joseph. Thank you, Michael.

MARTY Can I see the ring?

MICHAEL Pass it on.

The ring will be passed around the group during the following.

LEWIS What are you going to do with it?

MICHAEL Give it to Eugene. (*The group reacts.*) That was a joke, Jesus! I'm going to send the ring back. I just wanted to show it to you.

LEWIS If someone took our picture right now, I wonder if they would know we were gay men. I mean, look at us. I pass. At least, I think I pass.

MARTY Why do you want to?

LEWIS I didn't say that.

JOSEPH If someone *did* take our picture, I wonder if they would know which ones were the group and which one was the therapist?

MARTY Not you certainly.

GORDON That wasn't kind, Marty.

MARTY I still have issues with Joseph.

JOSEPH I wonder if they would know which ones of us had experienced great loss in the past seven or eight years? Does our grief show?

MARTY Is that how long we've been doing this? And I still don't have a boyfriend?

LEWIS Which ones had big dicks? That was a joke, Gordon.

MARTY A very inappropriate one, Lewis. No wonder Dennis left you.

MICHAEL Which ones had AIDS or were HIV?

JOSEPH Which ones were rich, which ones were just eking out a living?

MARTY Which ones were happy, which ones were on antidepressants?

PAT (*the one in the Vassar sweatshirt*) Which ones of us had slept together?

GORDON Okay, that tears it. You know sleeping together is against group rules, Pat.

PAT It was a fantasy. I haven't slept with anyone.

GORDON Even better. If we've learned nothing else, we've learned that our fantasies are the key to self-understanding. Who in the group do you want to sleep with, Pat?

PAT Don't make me do this, Gordon. Not in our last session. I'll tell you after Labor Day.

GORDON We can't wait to Labor Day.

LEWIS He wants to sleep with you, Gordon.

GORDON He has good taste. Come on, Pat.

PAT I want to sleep with Kurt.

KURT (*the one with the activist T-shirt*) I don't want to play this game.

PAT It's not a game.

KURT Sleep with someone else. Sleep with Marty.

MARTY   Please, do!

PAT   I knew this would happen, Gordon.

GORDON   Deal with it, Kurt.

KURT   Make him deal with it.

GORDON   He's trying to. He needs your help.

KURT   I don't want to.

GORDON   Look at each other. Now tell Kurt what you find attractive about him, Pat.

PAT   I like his nose. I think it's very sexy. The way it . . .

GORDON   Talk to Kurt, Pat, not us.

PAT   I like your eyes. They shine sometimes, even when they're sad. I like your hands. The veins in them. You have a man's hands. I like your sense of humor. I like your nose. I already said that. I like your eyelashes. I like your tattoo and wonder when you got it.

JOSEPH   This sucks.

EVERYONE   Ssshh!

PAT   I like the way you're kind to people in group and don't jump all over them when they say something out of line. You can be very gentle. I remember how you were when Gordon's father died and you hugged him when he started crying in front of the group and held him until he stopped. I like how you've always got a cause, how you're always trying to change things and make them better. You inspire me. (*to Gordon*) I don't know, Gordon, stuff like that.

GORDON   Talk to him, Kurt. Give him something back.

KURT I like your honesty.

PAT Thank you.

KURT I like the fact you never miss.

PAT You mean group?

KURT You're always here. I can count on you. That's very important.

PAT What else am I gonna do on a Wednesday night?

KURT I like your smile. It's very sweet.

PAT Thank you.

GORDON Anything else?

KURT I hope your generation doesn't go through what mine did.

PAT You're not so old.

KURT Just have a good life.

PAT I'm sorry you're positive.

KURT I'm not. I used to be but I'm not sorry anymore. I'm going to be fine.

GORDON Look at him, Kurt.

PAT I love you.

KURT I love you, too.

Some of the men begin to hold hands, probably without even being aware that they are. There is a silence. Then:

GORDON Have a great summer, gentlemen.

The group starts to disband.

LEWIS   You're all welcome in P-town!

JOSEPH   Where are you going to be, Gordon?

GORDON   The Berkshires, where else? The house is finally paid for. We are mortgage-free. I'm going to stand on our porch with a shotgun and let Ryan feed me to death.

MICHAEL   Anyone going to the subway?

JOSEPH   Subway? We're taking a cab tonight. Didn't you hear Gordon? We're cured through Labor Day.

MICHAEL   What are we going to do with our Wednesday nights?

JOSEPH   I'm sure you'll think of something, Michael.

LEWIS   You should start by thinking about your wedding.

JOSEPH   And why none of us was invited.

MARTY   I was. It's at the Waldorf.

MICHAEL   Eugene wants to keep it small.

Michael, JOSEPH, *Lewis and* MARTY *go.*

KURT   I'll see you in September, Pat.

PAT   I know you will.

KURT   Thanks.

He goes. Only Gordon and Pat remain.

GORDON   Are you okay?

PAT   Sure.

GORDON   Get the light when you go. Have a good summer, Pat.

He goes. Pat begins to sing a Madonna song and dance to it all by himself. KURT returns.

KURT I forgot my jacket, excuse me.

PAT I was dancing.

KURT Your secret is safe with me. I do the same thing when I think nobody's watching. I'll dance myself right out the window one day if I'm not careful.

PAT Don't do that!

KURT You're going to meet the right man and you're going to be very happy together. You're going to have long healthy lives.

PAT I am?

KURT Trust me, I know these things. Have a great summer. I'll see you in September.

He goes. Pat resumes the song and dance. Transition.

THE WEDDING—FINALE

The entire company reassembles in its original wedding ceremony positions.

VOICE Knowing the joy which accompanies your love for one another and firmly believing in the fulfillment of a lifetime together, do you take each other to be spouses for life?

EUGENE'S VOICE We do.

MICHAEL'S VOICE We do.

BERNIE I found the check.

CARL Good. Sshh.

BERNIE It was in the other pocket.

VOICE Do you both promise to bring faith, hope and joy to your union?

EUGENE'S VOICE We do.

MICHAEL'S VOICE We do.

VOICE Will you, Eugene, have Michael to be united in marriage?

EUGENE'S VOICE I will.

MARCUS (*to Perry*) I will, too.

VOICE And do you have some words for him, Eugene?

EUGENE'S VOICE Michael, I am the luckiest person in the world.

VOICE Will you, Michael, have Eugene to be united in marriage?

MICHAEL'S VOICE I will.

CARL (*to Bernie*) It's not too late for us to do this. A double wedding would make the *Times*.

VOICE And do you have some words also, Michael, for Eugene?

MICHAEL'S VOICE When I look into your eyes, I feel such a profound wonder, Eugene.

VOICE Please join hands and repeat after me.

Marcus and Perry join hands. So do Carl and Bernie.

VOICE (*cont.*) I, Eugene, take you, Michael, to be my spouse, to have and to hold from this day forward, for better, for worse, for richer, for poorer, to love and to cherish forever.

EUGENE'S VOICE I, Eugene, take you, Michael . . .

Etc., etc. At the same time as the wedding vows are being repeated we hear the following exchanges:

MARTY (*low to Aaron*) I know things about one of the grooms from group therapy that would make your hair stand on end but my lips are sealed. I'm sorry, you're crying.

AARON My partner and I didn't get to do this.

MARTY I'm sorry.

AARON We should have done it anyway.

MARTY I'm Marty, by the way.

AARON Aaron.

MARTY Hello, Aaron. Pleased to meet you.

VOICE I, Michael, take you, Eugene, to be my spouse, to have and to hold from this day forward, for better, for worse, for richer, for poorer, to love and cherish forever.

MICHAEL'S VOICE I, Michael, take you, Eugene—

Etc., etc. Again, as the wedding vows are being repeated, we hear the following exchanges:

MARCUS It's the babysitter.

He answers his cell phone.

FRITZ (*leaning in toward Paul*) Hi.

PAUL Hi.

FRITZ Fritz.

PAUL Paul.

FRITZ Hi.

PAUL Hi.

Marcus is off the cell phone.

PERRY What did he say?

MARCUS He asked if his boyfriend could come over.

PERRY I hope you told him no.

PAUL You want to get something after this?

FRITZ "I do."

VOICE I now pronounce you married. Gentlemen, you may kiss your spouse. Michael and Eugene, will you have your first dance as a married couple?

The piano man starts playing. At first the men watch Michael and EUGENE dance their first dance as marrieds in the space directly in front of them.

BERNIE *(calling out to them)* Good luck!

CARL *Mazel tov!*

MARCUS You're looking good, you two!

PAUL Aren't you supposed to toss the bouquet or something?

MARTY Bring him to group next time, Michael! He's a doll.

CARL *(to Bernie)* You want to dance?

BERNIE But I lead!

Now Bernie and Carl begin to dance.

MARCUS Look at them, Perry.

PERRY They're getting there.

MARCUS   Go cut in. Go on, ask him.

PERRY   He's my father!

MARCUS   Then I will. (*he approaches Bernie*) Dad?

Marcus dances with Bernie. Perry dances with Carl. Marty turns to Aaron.

MARTY   Would you care to dance?

AARON   Thanks, but I think I'll sit this one out.

Fritz and Paul look at one another.

PAUL   It's not exactly my music.

FRITZ   Mine either. Let's just do our thing.

They work something out between them. They look good together. Carl and Bernie are waltzing. Perry and Marcus are doing something a little more contemporary. Fritz and Paul are making it all up. Everyone but Marty and Aaron is dancing. The lights are beginning to fade.

End of Play

DEUCE

Deuce was originally produced on Broadway by Scott Rudin, Stuart Thompson, Maberry Theatricals, The Shubert Organization (Gerald Schoenfeld: Chairman; Philip J. Smith: President; Robert E. Wankel: Executive Vice President), Roger Berlin, Debra Black, Bob Boyett, Susan Dietz and Daryl Roth.

Deuce received its World premiere at The Music Box Theater, New York, May 6, 2007. It was directed by Michael Blakemore; the set design was by Peter J. Davison; the costume design was by Ann Roth; the lighting design was by Mark Henderson; the video and projection design by Sven Ortel; the sound design was by Paul Charlier; the production stage manager was Steven Beckler; and the company manager was Brig Berney. The cast was as follows:

AN ADMIRER Michael Mulheren

MIDGE BARKER Marian Seldes

LEONA MULLEN Angela Lansbury

RYAN BECKER Brian Haley

KELLY SHORT Joanna P. Adler

Tennis Scoring

A tennis match consists of sets, games, points.

Tennis scoring proceeds in points from love (or zero) to 15, 30, and 40. If both players have scored three points, the score is described as "deuce." When the score remains tied, it is described as "deuce," no matter how many points have been played. The player who scores the first point after deuce has the "advantage." If the player with the advantage loses the point, the score is deuce once again. If the player with the advantage wins the point, that player wins the game.

A match (in women's tennis) is won by the player who wins two of three sets.

The four Grand Slam tournaments are the most important tennis events of the year in terms of world ranking points, tradition, prize money awarded, and public attention. They are the Australian Open, the French Open, the U.S. Open, and Wimbledon. A singles player or doubles team that wins all four titles in the same year is said to have achieved the Grand Slam.

Grandstands. Tennis match in progress. We can hear the sounds of the ball being vigorously whacked back and forth. Two women follow the volleying until the umpire calls "Thirty-forty". Their heads turn at each stroke with perfect synchronicity. AN ADMIRER appears and stands watching them. They cannot see him, no matter where or how close he stands to them. Their heads continue to swivel in time to the volleying of the tennis ball as he speaks to us admiringly.

UMPIRE   Ladies and Gentlemen. Quiet Please! Players are ready.

AN ADMIRER   Look at them. I've watched these two from a distance for years—sometimes from way up there and sometimes from courtside—but what have I seen? Even this close, it's not easy. I look, I see—but I want to know them, understand them, remember them as they are and were. I want to see this game through their eyes.

UMPIRE (*off*)   Deuce!

LEONA MULLEN   The little Czech girl is good.

MIDGE BARKER   She's not Czech.

LEONA   Her name is Czech.

MIDGE   All their names are something now. She's from southern California. And if she's not from southern California she's from Florida.

We hear the sound of a tennis ball being served with a resounding thwack!

MIDGE (*cont.*)   None of them are from where it sounds like anymore.

UMPIRE   Advantage Sawallisch.

LEONA   Well done, young woman! What's her name?

MIDGE Sawallisch.

LEONA Well done, Sawallisch!

MIDGE She endorses things.

LEONA What sort of things?

MIDGE Tennis shoes, tennis costumes, tennis racquets, soft drinks, credit cards, the kitchen sink—that sort of stuff.

LEONA Good for her. I wish they'd asked us.

Sounds of the ball being served.

MIDGE I'm glad they didn't.

LEONA Why?

MIDGE We would have said yes.

LEONA We would not. Now we would, maybe, but not then. We were very pure.

UMPIRE Deuce!

LEONA We didn't agree about many things but we were unanimous about that.

MIDGE Not to worry. No one's going to ask us now.

LEONA We don't know that. Those women in the "What becomes a legend most?" advertising campaign were hardly in the flush of youth. I can see us posing together in matching minks.

Sound of ball being served.

MIDGE Those women were movie stars.

LEONA We were tennis stars. Huge, huge tennis stars.

MIDGE It's not the same thing.

LEONA It is now.

MIDGE Not really.

LEONA Well, almost.

UMPIRE Advantage Sawallisch!

MIDGE Tennis will always be caviar to the masses.

LEONA You always said that.

MIDGE It's true.

LEONA Well it's not like wrestling, if that's what you mean.

MIDGE It's not like baseball or football or basketball either.

LEONA What about what's-his-name? You know, the one with the backhand who's always changing his shirt for the photographers during the changeovers?

MIDGE That one!

LEONA His picture is everywhere.

MIDGE Of course it is. He's an exhibitionist.

LEONA He was on TV last night shilling for Viagra. What does Viagra have to do with tennis? I should think it would interfere with his game. We should have changed our shirts during the changeovers. That would have given them something to write home about. Women's chests are much more interesting than men's and we don't have to shave them for the camera.

Sounds of ball being served.

MIDGE Men have always had the advantage in that department and they always will. You know what they say: *plus ca change, plus c'est la meme chose.*

LEONA Not in Pittsburgh they didn't.

UMPIRE Deuce!

MIDGE Whoever came up with that slogan "You've come a long way, baby", you can be sure it wasn't a woman.

LEONA It was a man in an advertising agency trying to get more women to smoke themselves to death.

MIDGE Some of us almost did.

LEONA I don't think they even make that brand anymore. I never liked them. I was always sneaking Lucky Strikes when the sponsors weren't looking.

MIDGE My excuse has always been we didn't know then what we know now about tobacco.

LEONA Yes, we did. They just paid us enough money to pretend we didn't.

MIDGE They got their money's worth. We played some good tennis. We're going to die from something but it's not going to be that.

Sounds of ball being served.

LEONA Those first women's pro tennis tours changed everything. Without us, those two would still be little girls with racquets that were too big for them.

UMPIRE Advantage, Sawallisch!

MIDGE It wasn't the racquets that were too big for us. It was the dreams.

LEONA Let's not rehash anything. Let's enjoy this occasion— relish it, even. If not, let's at least keep it at our Christmas card and occasional phone call level. I didn't leave an air-conditioned condo in the desert to be reminded of anything unpleasant.

MIDGE I don't mean to be unpleasant, Leona.

LEONA I don't want to look back and I don't want to look ahead. I want to watch two attractive newcomers show their stuff and then I want to bask in the accolades that are coming our way—well deserved accolades, I hope you agree. Now if you have a bug up your ass about anything, Midge, please keep it to yourself. I am happy and I am healthy. At our age, that's a lot.

MIDGE What did I say?

Sounds of ball being served.

LEONA It was your tone. It was wistful. I have enough wist for a lifetime.

Back to the game.

UMPIRE Game, Sawallisch.

LEONA Damn, my little Czech is good. She reminds me of me at her age. She's got balls. I like that. You can't get anywhere anymore without balls. I had balls.

MIDGE Is that what you called them?

The women turn back to the tennis. At the same time, we will see them on large television monitors in a very tight two-shot.

MALE TV COMMENTATOR (RYAN) Our cameras have found two veritable tennis legends in the stands: Margaret "Midge" Barker and Leona Mullen. Can we pull in tighter on them? I want our viewers to get a good look at these two Grand Masters.

FEMALE TV COMMENTATOR (KELLY) Leona Mullen and Margaret Barker are arguably the two greatest doubles players in the history of women's tennis. They are here today as guests of the U.S. Open in recognition of their outstanding contribution to the sport and their roles as trailblazing female athletes.

RYAN This is quite an historic occasion, getting these two former champions back together for a last hurrah.

KELLY When I was still playing, Ryan—

RYAN My colleague in the booth, Kelly Short, is twice a U.S. Open runner-up!

KELLY —I didn't just worship them. I wanted to be them. Growing up, I had their picture on my bedroom wall right next to Martina's.

RYAN Listen, I felt the same way. When I was still playing, Kelly—

KELLY Ryan Becker, Davis Cup team player three consecutive years but too modest to tell you himself.

RYAN Seriously, every time I played at the Open and I walked down the hall of fame out to center court, I'd see their pictures, their trophies, their incredible record of wins. Awesome. Just awesome.

KELLY Maybe we should tell our viewers which one is which.

RYAN That's Midge Barker on the left and Leona Mullen on the right.

Checks quickly with voice in his headset.

RYAN (*cont.*) I'm sorry, Ms. Mullen is on the left and Ms. Barker is on the right.

The crowd lets out a collective groan.

KELLY That was a sloppy unforced error by the French woman. She seems to be running out of steam.

RYAN I think she's losing concentration, Kelly, not stamina.

KELLY Whatever she's losing, it's no way to win the U.S. Open.

RYAN Midge Barker and Leona Mullen didn't get to where they are in the history of this game playing that kind of tennis. Shall we get back to the game?

LEONA *is looking across the stadium and up at the furthest reaches of it and for the first time taking in its size.*

LEONA The size of these new stadiums!

MIDGE Thousands and thousand of seats. From here to eternity!

LEONA When did tennis get so greedy?

MIDGE Tennis would say so popular.

LEONA I'd get a nosebleed sitting up there. They must be the cheap seats.

MIDGE There are no cheap seats. That's why they have those huge television screens everywhere: so people can actually see the game.

LEONA We had our bad days—

MIDGE Very few, Lee.

LEONA But we never disgraced ourselves in a thirty-foot close-up.

MIDGE And we lived to tell the tale.

LEONA (*with a mock gesture*) We who are about to die salute you.

MIDGE You're seventy-what now, Lee?

LEONA That was a joke, Midge.

MIDGE I know. I just turned seventy-two.

LEONA Good for you. I just turned thirty-five. A very mature thirty-five, I told a journalist who felt the need to ask.

MIDGE I embrace my age. I love it, I love it, I love it.

LEONA That's a goddamn lie.

MIDGE Well of course it is—and I don't appreciate the profanity.

LEONA You never did.

MIDGE I've never understood people who have difficulty admitting their age.

LEONA I admit it every morning when I drag myself out of bed and look in the bathroom mirror. It's reason enough to stop brushing your teeth. I gave up flossing years ago. I don't have to admit my age to anyone else.

MIDGE I know how old you are.

LEONA Then why did you ask? Either of us embraces her age anymore and she'll be dead.

MIDGE I didn't know this would be so awkward.

LEONA It doesn't have to be.

MIDGE Ten years is a long time.

LEONA Since we last saw each other? That's not possible.

MIDGE Miami. The WTA conference.

LEONA That wasn't ten years. It couldn't have been.

MIDGE It was.

LEONA Lord have mercy!

MIDGE I know. *Où sont les neiges d'antan?* Where are the snows of yesteryear?

LEONA That used to annoy the hell out of me. The French *and* the translation.

MIDGE I know. That's probably why I did it.

LEONA If you want to revisit the old days, you're on your own. I don't want to wallow. Besides, I've become a very private person in retirement.

MIDGE You always were, Lee.

LEONA Listen to you, Miss Still Waters Run Deep!

MIDGE Not anymore. In Blue Harbor I'm known as the Bitch on Wheels.

LEONA You always were a lousy driver.

MIDGE I don't think they're referring to my driving, Lee.

LEONA I know, Midge.

UMPIRE Game and first set, Sawallisch.

LEONA Do you know what you're going to say?

MIDGE Of course, I do. I've got it right here. It took me weeks. Don't you?

LEONA No, I'm going to wing it.

MIDGE That's leaving rather a lot to spur of the moment inspiration, wouldn't you say?

LEONA That's how I played tennis. You were the one with the game plan.

MIDGE You had your strategies, too.

LEONA Maybe I won't say anything.

MIDGE They expect something from you, Lee.

LEONA Sometimes a simple "thank you" is enough.

MIDGE That's not my experience. People like gush.

LEONA I'm out of gush and there's no more where it came from.

MIDGE No one's asking you to do cartwheels, Lee. Just a simple expression of gratitude in five hundred-or-so grateful, graceful words.

LEONA I'd rather do the cartwheels.

MIDGE I have an extra pen and paper, if you think of something to say.

LEONA (*not a bad imitation of a dog's bark*) Woof-woof!

MIDGE (*immediately closing down*) Fine. Make a fool of yourself.

LEONA (*delighted with herself*) Woof-woof! It still works, after all these years!

MIDGE I said fine, Lee.

UMPIRE   Resume play!

LEONA   No one likes a dog with a bone, Midge. If I ever get that way, I hope you'll do the same thing: Woof-woof me until I stop.

MIDGE   All I asked is what you were going to say.

LEONA   And I told you I didn't know. And then you turned into a rat terrier worrying a bone because you didn't like my answer.

MIDGE   Have it your way, Lee, you usually did.

LEONA   What was that?

MIDGE   Nothing.

UMPIRE   Second set, Lanvin-Grillet to serve.

Sounds of ball being served.

UMPIRE *(cont.)*   Fifteen-love.

LEONA   The umpire's attractive, don't you think?

Sounds of ball being served.

MIDGE   I've always tried to give people what they want.

LEONA   How well I know.

MIDGE   It's how I was brought up.

LEONA   There's no limit to what people want.

MIDGE   So I am learning.

UMPIRE   Fifteen-all.

LEONA   Maybe you're just a nicer person than I am, Midge, and it has nothing to do with our childhoods or any of that

I-was-traumatized-when-my-father-beat-me-with-a-tennis racquet-if-I-double-faulted-when-I-was-seven claptrap.

MIDGE You never told me that.

LEONA Because it never happened! I was making a point. You were always the nice one.

MIDGE Everyone is born nice. They become something else along the way.

LEONA That's true. "What a lovely child, Frau Hitler, may I hold him?"

MIDGE Don't flatter yourself, Lee, he was a fiend of history. Even at your worst, you were hardly that.

LEONA Despite my best efforts. Thank you, Midge.

MIDGE And I don't think anyone, ever, in the history of our sport has been scarred by a parent beating them with a racquet. Gently struck on the behind maybe but not beaten.

LEONA You know how I feel about psychotherapy. A total waste. Tennis should be a duel of muscles, wits, and nerves—not neuroses. I can't see that all their therapy has done anything for my three.

MIDGE How are they?

LEONA Getting on. Gordon, the baby, just joined AARP. I'm not supposed to notice. How are your little monsters?

MIDGE I'm a grandmother again. Three boys, three girls now. One of them was born with spina bifida.

LEONA I'm sorry.

MIDGE But the others are fine. Outstanding in fact.

LEONA I'm very sorry.

Pause. They stop watching the match.

UMPIRE Deuce!

MIDGE Do you believe we stopped playing tennis more than thirty years ago?

LEONA I stopped counting thirty years ago.

MIDGE Do you miss it?

LEONA Somedays something fierce; others, not at all.

RYAN You know, Kelly, maybe a word about today's players would remind our viewers just how much tennis, especially women's tennis, has changed since the glory years of our two guests of honor today.

KELLY Tennis was a homegrown affair but not anymore. Giselle Lanvin-Grillet was born in Corsica to an Italian-Croatian mother and a French-Basque father.

RYAN Wasn't Napoleon from Corsica, Kelly?

KELLY It doesn't say in my notes.

RYAN I'm pretty sure he was.

KELLY When Giselle's parents discovered her natural athletic abilities, they enrolled her in a tennis academy outside of Marseille where her skills were quickly recognized by her coaches who arranged for a scholarship to a tennis training center in the United States.

RYAN San Diego. She was just thirteen.

KELLY Since then, Giselle's rise to the eighth ranking player in women's tennis at the age of nineteen has astonished tennis fans everywhere.

RYAN I was nineteen when I won my first major title.

KELLY Her earnings last year totaled close to two million dollars and her numerous TV endorsements have made her a household name and face to millions.

RYAN I love her Fiesta Celebrity cruise ship commercial! Sure makes me want to travel.

KELLY Should Giselle win this year's U.S. Open, it would be her first major win in a skyrocketing career. So far she's been luckier scoring endorsement contracts than Grand Slam titles.

RYAN It's never hurt to be a looker.

KELLY I think your tennis wins should come before your celebrity endorsements. That's true old time tennis grit sitting down there courtside.

RYAN You can say that again.

UMPIRE Let! First service.

LEONA Don't you think he's kind of dreamy?

MIDGE In a Tyrone Power sort of way.

LEONA What was wrong with Tyrone Power?

MIDGE We never had the same taste in men.

LEONA Lucky for us we didn't. We wouldn't have lasted six weeks.

Sounds of ball being served.

MIDGE I think we're heading for a third set. At the rate they're going in this one, my little Frenchie is going to trounce your little Czech.

LEONA   I didn't know we'd chosen sides.

MIDGE   Of course we have. You can't be indifferent to the struggle between two players. One of those young women will trump the other. It would be totally unnatural not to care which.

LEONA   Well, I'm switching my allegiance to the little French girl. I've turned on the Czech.

MIDGE   Why?

LEONA   She's all technique, no heart.

MIDGE   That's how they're taught.

LEONA   Tennis robots. You can't tell one from the other. We were distinct. Even as a team, we were very different players.

MIDGE   You sure you want the French girl? I'm surprised. You never liked the French.

LEONA   I still don't. The French think they invented tennis.

MIDGE   I believe they did.

LEONA   That's no excuse.

MIDGE   We can't both be rooting for the same player.

LEONA   Of course we can.

MIDGE   That's no fun.

LEONA   You still make so many rules for yourself!

MIDGE   Then I'll take the little Czech girl from southern California who endorses things.

UMPIRE   Advantage Lanvin-Grillet!

MIDGE   Do we know if she's a lesbian?

LEONA   Which one?

MIDGE   The Czech—but I suppose either of them while we're at it.

LEONA   It's impossible to tell anymore.

MIDGE   So many of them are now.

UMPIRE   Game, Lanvin-Grillet.

LEONA   Everyone thought we were lesbians.

MIDGE   Because we were so good. But now even some of the really poor players are lesbians. It used to be a pledge of excellence.

LEONA   The men wanted all the women to be lesbians so they could label women's tennis a freak show. I think they were disappointed when it turned out that only some of them actually were. They couldn't accept women wanting to play as hard or win as much as they did. No, not win, but to care so much *about* winning.

MIDGE   Tennis was a genteel pastime for rich white women *after* they'd cooked a meal and put the children to bed. We were pioneers.

LEONA   Good for us.

MIDGE   How did they get away with it for so long?

LEONA   We let them.

A roar of delight and/or dismay from the crowd. MIDGE *covers her eyes.*

LEONA (*cont.*)   We've got a streaker.

UMPIRE   Security to court!

LEONA   He doesn't have much to write home about, does he? We should have brought our binoculars.

MIDGE   Tell me when he's gone.

LEONA   Obviously, he doesn't think she's a lesbian.

MIDGE   How do you mean?

LEONA   What would be the point of streaking a lesbian?

MIDGE   What is the point of streaking anyone? Is he gone?

LEONA   Yes.

Midge uncovers her eyes. The streaker is still on the playing court.

MIDGE   You said he was gone!

LEONA   He was gone and then he came back. Were we ever streaked?

MIDGE   No, thank God. A penis would have completely thrown my game.

LEONA   I guess they really did think we were lesbians.

MIDGE   What if we were? That's what I always said: "What if we were, Lee, what if we were!"

LEONA   No, you didn't, Midge. You used to get into a terrible tizzy over it. We both did. My God, I remember painting each other's nails before a match. Wearing make-up, earrings! They had us running around like chickens with our heads cut off for a time there trying to prove we were real women, whatever the hell that means. We were both so afraid of being seen for what we really were: damn good athletes.

MIDGE Do you remember that women's tournament in DC?

LEONA What did they call it? The Ball Busters Tour. I'm still cringing.

MIDGE What were we supposed to do? Play in high heels?

LEONA I look back at that period with such shame. What were we thinking? It was every woman for herself and the dykes be damned.

MIDGE We were terrible to the women we thought were lesbians. One of them would ask me for a drink after a match and I'd come up with the most amazing excuses not to. I told what's-her-name, you know who I mean . . .

LEONA The one who had such a crush on you?

MIDGE I told her I didn't drink and I didn't like people who did. Just the thought of being seen with her in a hotel cocktail lounge—her drinking beer out of a bottle—was enough to send me to my room alone and order from room service. We knew what was happening and pretended we didn't. We were complicit, Lee. You're supposed to contradict me.

LEONA I can't. I used to watch those women in the locker room and feel so superior. It was too scary to acknowledge we both wanted the same thing: to play the best tennis we could. She died, you know, your admirer. Mary Giordano!, it just came back to me, her name. Just last November. I saw her six months before at a USTA conference in San Francisco. She was with her partner. She didn't look well. That look people get when they're dying and there's no pretending they're not. "I'm dying, Lee" she said, first thing. She was very direct about it. We had a drink and reminisced about the good old days, which really weren't all that good we decided. Her partner didn't seem that interested. Most civilians aren't. She kept asking me about the price of real estate in Arizona. I think she was already planning her future without Mary. She seemed glad when we took our leave. The partner, I mean. Mary and I, we could have gone on for hours. There was no wall between us anymore.

MIDGE   Did she ask for me?

LEONA   What do you think?

MIDGE   What did you tell her?

LEONA   I told her you always thought she had the best net game of anyone in professional tennis, man or woman.

MIDGE   It's true, I did.

LEONA   I think that made her very happy.

MIDGE   There was a time when I thought you might be a lesbian.

LEONA   There were times when I wished I were! The road could get awfully lonely.

MIDGE   Did you ever think I might be one?

LEONA   You? A lesbian? Don't be ridiculous.

MIDGE   It's all right, you can tell me.

LEONA   It never even crossed my mind.

MIDGE   I wasn't good enough to be a lesbian?

LEONA   Now you're insulted!

MIDGE   Now they could write I was a transsexual crack addict on steroids and it wouldn't faze me.

LEONA   If you were, they'd probably beg you to come out of retirement. It's become a circus. We didn't need giant television screens. We argued whether a ball was in or out; we didn't let a goddamn machine decide for us. I knew when I hit a good serve. I didn't need another goddamn machine to tell me how many goddamn miles an hour it was going. This was a great sport. I weep for tennis. Men's tennis. Women's tennis. I weep for the entire game. There were giants, Midge.

MIDGE   We were giants, Lee.

LEONA   I find that very humbling. We stood center court at Wimbledon and curtsied to the Royal Box. Princess Margaret was sitting in it. We were both certain she was quite drunk. They gave us a silver cup for our efforts.

MIDGE   Later that night we got a little tight ourselves and Cary Grant asked us both to dance at the Curzon Club in Mayfair. Of course we were both married and he was, too, and we all left with our respective spouses but I don't think it gets much better than that, do you?

LEONA   Only a little bit.

MIDGE   And now look at us.

LEONA   I was hoping you weren't going to say that.

MIDGE   How the mighty have fallen.

LEONA   We haven't fallen. We've aged, gotten older, through no fault of our own. It happens to every goddamn one of us and that's the goddamn truth.

MIDGE Truth is not a pejorative word. There's nothing "goddamn" about it. (And I really don't appreciate the profanity, Lee.) It's the truth, whether we like it or not—the truth couldn't care less. The truth is I liked it better when we had to wear white on the court and no one even dreamed of endorsing things. But so what? So their F-word fucking what?

LEONA You can't say "the F word" and then say "fucking" in the same sentence. You defeat your own purpose.

MIDGE We played because we loved the game, not because we got paid for it.

LEONA I loved it even more after we started getting paid. I put the founding of the Womens Tennis Association right up there with the Emancipation Proclamation.

MIDGE People should love what they do.

LEONA People should be good at what they do.

MIDGE I gave my life to tennis.

LEONA We both did.

UMPIRE Forty-love.

They watch the match in silence, their heads turning in perfect unison as the ball is volleyed back and forth.

UMPIRE (*cont.*) Forty-fifteen.

ADMIRER I only saw them play a couple of times in the twilight of their careers. An Open at Forest Hills; Roland Garros, the French Open; a killer match in San Francisco. But once would have been enough. It was all there, everytime they played: the unexplainable, the inexplicable genius of how they did what they had chosen to do with their lives. It took my breath away. It still does.

The person speaking these words, remember, is not visible to Leona and Midge.

ADMIRER (*cont.*)   To have seen Midge Barker serve! Tossing the ball high over head, seeing it hang there suspended for what seemed like the briefest of eternities, before the fearless smash of her racquet and another ace whizzed by her opponent. And to watch Leona Mullen cover the net like a tigress—snarling, raging, hissing, reaching to make returns a man twice her size wouldn't have tried—all the time playing tennis that dared anyone else to attempt it. And to see them play together! Was one of them better than the other? Probably. I'm glad we never found out.

UMPIRE   Forty-thirty.

MIDGE   It's going to be over in two sets after all.

LEONA   No, my Frenchie's gonna pull it together and we'll be in for a third.

KELLY   During our last break, we neglected to tell our viewers about our other player today.

RYAN   To her fans, and she's got a lot of them, we're sorry.

KELLY   Ute-Lynne Sawallisch was born in Cracow, the only daughter of a respected judge and an opera singer, a noted contralto. When her parents separated, Ute-Lynne was brought to the United States on a tennis scholarship. She was 10 years old.

RYAN   I was ten when I picked up my first racquet.

KELLY   Ute-Lynne (or Willy as her friends call her) is perhaps the most controversial figure in women's tennis.

RYAN   And not because she's an outspoken environmentalist. Along with her partner, a gold medal gymnast, the two have been active in the Green Movement and have adopted three children from Central America.

KELLY   Still, her flawless technique has won her almost as many fans as her bad temper lost them.

RYAN   You're talking about the incident at Wimbledon this year?

KELLY   It was more than an incident, Ryan. She was at match point when she was disqualified for slapping a ball girl who distracted her serve. She said the twelve-year-old yawned.

RYAN   That fierce Polish temperament of hers is a liability as much as it is an advantage.

KELLY   Unlike her endorsement-heavy opponent. Ute-Lynne has won the French Open and twice made it to the finals at Wimbledon.

RYAN   Nevertheless, the easy popularity Lanvin-Grillet enjoys continues to elude her.

KELLY   Oh, that was a big point!

UMPIRE   Game, Lanvin-Grillet! Code violation. Audible obscenity. Warning Sawallisch.

The Admirer makes himself visible to Midge and Leona as an
AUTOGRAPH SEEKER.

AUTOGRAPH SEEKER   Could I trouble you ladies for an autograph?

LEONA We've been recognized, Midge! I hope you have a pen.

AUTOGRAPH SEEKER Yes, I do.

LEONA Well, that's something! I can't tell you the number of times I've been asked for my autograph by someone who doesn't have a pen. It's very annoying.

AUTOGRAPH SEEKER I can imagine.

LEONA Or it's a tennis ball they want you to sign. Do you know how hard it is to write on a tennis ball?

MIDGE Mrs. Mullen is the WTA's first and original tennis martyr.

LEONA You didn't like it either, Midge. (*to autograph seeker*) You're exhausted after a match and you just want to get back to the hotel and into a hot tub and these people don't have a pen or the camera flash doesn't work.

MIDGE Like I said, it's a hard life.

LEONA (*laughing*) You're right. She's right. Where would you like me to sign?

AUTOGRAPH SEEKER Here's a new page.

LEONA An autograph book! Look, Midge. I didn't think people kept autograph books anymore.

AUTOGRAPH SEEKER It was my father's. He passed it on to me. He started this book when he was a teenager. He got all the greats of his day to sign it. Now it's up to me.

LEONA Is that May Sutton's signature? She was my coach's idol. He's got May Sutton in here, Midge.

AUTOGRAPH SEEKER My father saw her years after she'd retired, she was the guest of honor at an event such as this, I believe it was in the early seventies, just before she died, and he asked her for it. It was his pride and joy.

LEONA She was the first American to win Wimbledon.

AUTOGRAPH SEEKER I know. My Grandfather was there. He was a young man but he never forgot it. He was so proud to be an American that day.

MIDGE It was 1905. This was before we had tiebreakers. It went for three very long sets. They played almost four hours.

LEONA Midge is an encyclopedia of women's tennis. I just concentrated on winning. Ask her anything.

MIDGE 1905 was also the year the Australasian tennis championship was first held.

LEONA Australasian! You see what I mean? I would have said Australian. Most people would.

MIDGE It wouldn't be correct. It was renamed the Australian Championship in 1927.

LEONA Thank you, Midge.

AUTOGRAPH SEEKER My father had the pleasure of seeing you two win the U.S. Open on two separate occasions.

LEONA We won three.

AUTOGRAPH SEEKER He only saw two.

LEONA (*she can be charming*) Tell him that's no excuse.

AUTOGRAPH SEEKER He passed six years ago.

LEONA I'm sorry. I don't suppose you ever saw us play?

AUTOGRAPH SEEKER Forest Hills, the Open. You won in straight sets. I was seven years old and sat on my father's lap and got a terrible sunburn.

LEONA I'm liking your father more and more. (*seeing another familiar name in the autograph book*) Lili de Alvarez, 1928. She was a fashion plate on court and off and married a count.

MIDGE Rather like you.

LEONA I was never a fashion plate. (*to autograph seeker*) A dish, maybe, but not a plate.

MIDGE I was speaking about Kip.

LEONA (*to autograph seeker*) I married well, as they used to say.

MIDGE They still do, Leona.

LEONA I married the best.

AUTOGRAPH SEEKER I remember my father being very sad for you when Mr. Mullen passed.

LEONA Alice Marble, Pauline Betz, Sarah Palfrey Cooke— that's a name you don't hear much anymore. "Babe" Didrikson Zaharias! Southampton, New York, July 4, 1940.

MIDGE The "Babe"! I had her picture on my bedroom wall.

AUTOGRAPH SEEKER My father thought she was the greatest all-around female athlete of all time.

MIDGE Don't let Leona hear you say that.

LEONA I never considered her a real tennis player. She was a golf and track and field sort of woman. She dabbled in tennis.

MIDGE She dabbled in everything. She played baseball, she golfed, she played basketball. I saw her do a perfect jackknife off the thirty-meter platform in Miami. This was after she'd won two gold medals at the Olympics in 1932.

LEONA Exactly my point, she dabbled. Tennis is focus. Gertrude "Gorgeous Gussie" Moran! Imagine being remembered for how you dressed rather than how you played.

AUTOGRAPH SEEKER You two always looked great in your pictures. Very classic in your tennis whites.

MIDGE Thank you.

LEONA I liked a discreet touch of color. A ribbon, a bit of piping.

MIDGE Leona was our fashion rebel. I was more Grace Kelly. I still am.

LEONA All these names! Margaret Osborne. We liked her. Margaret Court. Maureen Connolly. Midge, here's Little Mo's autograph.

AUTOGRAPH SEEKER She wrote "Maureen Connolly a.k.a. Killer Connolly". Was she a killer?

MIDGE "Killer" was the press's name for her. When she got really serious about her game, they turned on her. They liked her more when she was "Little Mo"—all girlish tears and teenage giggles. In her day, it was unfeminine to win so consecutively.

AUTOGRAPH SEEKER Thank God for you feminists.

LEONA I was never a feminist. I was a woman who played tennis.

MIDGE Mrs. Mullen's always had difficulty with that particular "F" word. The other one she's fine with.

LEONA I didn't like the label. I liked the score at the end of two sets.

MIDGE But you're right, we owe the feminists a lot.

LEONA We owe Billie Jean King a lot and so does every name in this book *after* hers. (*to autograph seeker*) Now who do you want this to? You are . . . ?

AUTOGRAPH SEEKER That's all right. Just your name.

LEONA You sure? I'm in a signing mood.

AUTOGRAPH SEEKER Just your name and the date. I think it's purer that way.

Leona signs the autograph book. She hands the book to Midge.

MIDGE Where do you want me to sign? On the same page with Mrs. Mullen?

AUTOGRAPH SEEKER Please.

MIDGE Together forever!

LEONA Forever until Miss Barker decided she no longer wished to play with me.

MIDGE I'll still sign on the same page. It's how people are going to remember us.

LEONA Whether we like it or not.

AUTOGRAPH SEEKER Thank you, Miss Barker.

MIDGE Barker was my professional name. My married name is Cook.

AUTOGRAPH SEEKER   I'm sorry, Mrs. Cook.

MIDGE   I prefer Barker.

She signs book and returns it.

MIDGE (*cont.*)   Here you are. And we don't want to see it on eBay tonight!

AUTOGRAPH SEEKER   That, you won't. I will treasure this.

MIDGE   Take good care of it.

AUTOGRAPH SEEKER   You don't have to worry about that. As long as I'm around, this book is sacred. Congratulations. You truly deserve today. This is a great game. People like you made it better.

He goes.

MIDGE   I wasn't expecting that. Were you?

LEONA   Not for one second.

UMPIRE   Resume play!

Sound of a first serve. This time the two women do not bother to turn their heads to watch the ball being volleyed back and forth.

The Admirer stands apart and watches them.

ADMIRER   Thank you seems inadequate but finally it's all we have for one another. I can't physically touch or hold them. I'm not family. We can only end up fans of the people we admire. An autograph, a photo, our memory—they're all we have of people like these. When we're gone, they're gone, too.

He goes as the sound of a propeller airplane is heard droning high overhead.

LEONA   It's one of those goddamn flying advertisements. They shouldn't let these goddamn planes fly so near the stadium.

MIDGE   When did you start saying "goddamn" every other word?

LEONA   When I stopped going to church—and I don't say it every other word. But who has allowed this to happen to American tennis? Surely someone somewhere is responsible. They're playing on some synthetic surface with metal racquets the size of snow shoes and neon balls. I said it at the time they were introduced: Yellow balls are going to be the beginning of the end of tennis. Remember?

MIDGE   You've always blamed the balls.

LEONA   Listen to me: I sound like everything I never wanted to become. I get so angry at how everything has changed and then I get angry at myself for getting angry. Things change, I know that. Things are supposed to change. I know that, too. They should change. But couldn't those changes at least last for the rest of our lifetime?

MIDGE   I know, Lee, I know.

LEONA   Well, that will be over soon enough.

They turn and look at each other for the first time.

LEONA *(cont.)*   How are you, Midge, really?

MIDGE   I'm fine, Lee. How are you?

LEONA   I'm fine, too.

MIDGE   Really?

LEONA   Really.

MIDGE   Good, I'm glad.

LEONA   Me, too. I had a cancer scare but I'm fine now.

MIDGE   A cancer scare?

LEONA   It said "boo" and I said "boo" right back. I'm fine.

Sound of ball being served, four volleys, crowd response.

UMPIRE   Game, Lanvin-Grillet.

LEONA   My little French girl charges the net like there's no tomorrow. *Allons, cherie, allons!* What's her name?

MIDGE   Giselle something.

LEONA   *Allons, Giselle. Vive la France!*

MIDGE   She's from Orange County, Lee.

LEONA   Marvelous! Did you see that? Absolutely fearless. You either have an instinct for this game or you don't. You can talk about finesse till you're blue in the face but unless you're willing to improvise in the moment, you'll never be better than an also-ran.

MIDGE   I knew my Achilles' heel. Aphrodite's heel, I should say. The net—intractable and unforgiving as a brick wall. I always left the charging to you.

LEONA   With your serve, you didn't need a net game.

MIDGE   Everyone needs a net game. You never wanted to fix your service.

LEONA   That's not true, Midge. I tried very hard to.

MIDGE   Your toss was never high enough, Lee.

LEONA   I tossed it as high as I could.

MIDGE I lived in terror of your double-faulting.

LEONA No more than I.

MIDGE Well, not anymore I don't.

UMPIRE Love-thirty.

LEONA I knew one of us would bring up Australia sooner or later.

MIDGE It was the furthest thing from my mind, Lee.

LEONA There's hardly a day I don't think about it.

MIDGE I hope that's an exaggeration. We won enough majors for anyone. For any two women anyway. No, for any two anything.

LEONA We didn't win the Australian.

MIDGE We won the French five consecutive years; the U.S. Open three; and Wimbledon, four.

LEONA None of which are the Australian.

MIDGE Why are you fixed on a loss that occurred more than thirty years ago?

LEONA A loss occasioned by my double-faulting.

MIDGE Everything leads to a loss—every point in the game, every error, not just a single double-fault.

LEONA It was my double fault, not yours. You played brilliantly that day.

MIDGE We played brilliantly.

LEONA Until I double-faulted.

MIDGE It doesn't matter.

LEONA Yes, it does.

MIDGE It mattered then, I will concede that, but not anymore.

LEONA It still matters. It will always matter.

MIDGE Not to me.

LEONA I wanted the Australian. I wanted a Grand Slam.

MIDGE Well we didn't get the Australian. That's life. Between your aggressive journeys to the net and my devastating first serves, we did pretty well for ourselves, old girl.

LEONA I didn't want to stop when we did.

MIDGE I thought we should quit while we were ahead.

LEONA We had a couple of good years left.

MIDGE I wasn't so sure about that.

LEONA Well, we should have found out.

MIDGE I realize it was my decision, Leona.

LEONA Unfortunately, when you're part of a doubles team, every "my" decision is an "our" decision.

MIDGE You have me to blame.

LEONA I didn't say that. I put too many eggs in one basket. First you, then Kip.

MIDGE You could have tried your hand at singles.

LEONA Not after all those years as your partner. It would have been like starting all over again.

MIDGE I knew my limitations. You invented yours.

Sounds of the ball being volleyed. The women watch the game in silence a while.

KELLY While you've been enjoying some great tennis, my colleague and I have been Googling our guests of honor.

RYAN I knew they were good, Kelly, but this is incredible. Together, these two women won every Slam but the Australian. All of them more than once. The French Open, five titles, in as many consecutive years! Four Wimbledons, three U.S. Opens.

KELLY These are team doubles records they don't expect ever to be broken. On a more personal note, Midge Barker was born in New York City to a prominent Park Avenue family. She attended Vassar where she majored in political science.

RYAN An athlete with a college degree. I barely made it out of high school.

KELLY Leona Mullen's roots were less auspicious. She is the only daughter of a Pittsburgh Incline conductor who taught her how to hold her first tennis racket in a city park at the tender age of five. She attended Penn State but the lack of scholarships for female athletes in her day forced her to drop out after her freshman year in order to devote herself to tennis full-time.

RYAN Since they retired in 1974, both women have been living quietly in retirement. Leona Mullen in Tucson with her second husband, a developer, and Midge Barker in Blue Harbor, Maine.

KELLY Let me put them in some sort of historical context for you, Ryan. The struggles to establish the professional women's tennis circuit were heroic. For years, women weren't allowed to play professional tennis and when they were, the men had a twelve to one ratio advantage in prize money. It wasn't until 1973 that the Women's Tennis Association was established.

RYAN Before that, women played professional tennis almost for nothing, in other words?

KELLY They certainly weren't earning a living.

RYAN And now women earn. . . . what? Millions of dollars?

KELLY I won't categorically say my generation of players was better than their's—it's all relative, after all—but I think we hit harder and faster and certainly we had a more varied game than theirs. Frankly, Ryan, Leona and Midge's game seems quaint compared to the power of today's players.

MIDGE Do you think we could have taken these two, Lee?

LEONA Creamed them.

RYAN Today's tennis technology must be pretty bewildering to these wooden racquet-era players.

LEONA Helen Keller could have played tennis with a racquet that size. You just have to hold it out to hit the ball.

RYAN So let me ask you this, Kelly: Do you think tennis in general is better now than it was in their day?

KELLY If you're asking me is it more exciting? more competitive? is the level of play higher? the answer is yes.

RYAN I hear you. Absolutely.

KELLY But other than that, it's the same game. Get the ball over the net and past your opponent more times than she does. Work on your first serve and don't double-fault. It's still tennis.

Leona and Midge are still intently following the rally. Only now we can hear what sounds like a grunt each time the ball is hit.

LEONA What's that sound? Do you hear something? Is that them?

MIDGE They all grunt now.

LEONA We didn't grunt. Maybe an occasional "unh" but nothing like that. I would have been embarrassed to make a sound like that.

MIDGE I think it's part of their game. They practice their grunts along with their return of serve.

Midge stands up and takes off her sweater.

LEONA It's very unladylike.

MIDGE I can't believe you said that.

LEONA Neither can I.

MIDGE The wars we fought over that one word: lady!

LEONA Good wars.

MIDGE Important ones.

LEONA Did we win?

MIDGE I think so. Don't you?

LEONA Absolutely.

Sounds of ball being served and volley.

UMPIRE Deuce.

At once the lights fade on Midge and we see Leona in a tight spot of light.

LEONA Midge has grown much more beautiful with the
years. That happens to some women. Some men, too. It's as
if they've been refined by time and at last we see their true
selves. I remember when I was the looker. I was the one
people were looking at. Now Midge is. How does such a
thing happen? Has she led a better life than me? Probably. A
lot of people have led a better life than me but they don't
end up looking like Midge. There's a . . . what? . . . a grace,
a serenity in her face that was never there before. I wonder
if people recognize her still? When they see her on the
street or on an airplane do they say to themselves "That's
Midge Barker. God, she was good. How many Grand Slam
titles did those two win? Her and what's-her-name? A
dozen, at least, maybe more. They *were* women's tennis.
Women's doubles, anyway. What *was* the other one's
name?" Or do they merely think "That's an attractive older
woman. Wonderful carriage, terrific bone structure." Or do
they not see her at all? We become invisible as we grow
older. I wonder if Midge can remember the last time a
younger person—a waiter, a waitress, a check out person at
the market—really looked at her? Saw her. Took her in.
"You're talking to Leona Mullen," I want to say to young
people. "Look at her when she speaks to you. Look at
Leona Mullen. Look at me." I wonder if it happens to
Midge. It must. I am not invisible, goddamnit, look at me!

The lights up on Midge.

MIDGE Did you say something?

LEONA No.

UMPIRE Game and second set, Lanvin-Grillet.

At once the lights return to "normal."

MIDGE A third set!

LEONA What did I tell you?

MIDGE I love a good nail-biter. I'm not making any predictions. People always think I know who's going to win these things. I was sitting next to the nicest young man on the plane (nice *looking*, I mean, we hadn't spoken a word other than "excuse me" when I took my seat) when completely out of the blue, just like that, he said, "So who do you think is going to win the Open, Miss Barker?" He couldn't have been more than twenty and he'd recognized me. Well, you could have knocked me over with a feather. You must get that, too. Probably more than me. You were the one whose autograph everyone wanted or have their picture taken with. One sportswriter called me the *eminence grise* of women's tennis.

LEONA I thought they were paying you a compliment. Then I rushed home to look it up in the dictionary. An *eminence grise*—

MIDGE I know what an *eminence grise* is, Lee. It's hardly the sort of thing a young woman wants to be known as: another woman's *eminence grise*.

LEONA It was your own fault.

MIDGE Why are you so grumpy?

LEONA It's hot out here, I had a terrible flight but you're right. I'm sorry.

MIDGE Did you fly first class?

LEONA Of course I did.

MIDGE And you still had a terrible flight? I thought the whole

point of spending all that money was that you wouldn't
have a terrible flight.

LEONA I thought it was, too, but that was before flight 403
from Tucson.

MIDGE I think it's ridiculous to spend all that money for first
class. You know what they say: "Death doesn't care where
you're sitting when the plane goes down."

LEONA I thought the expression was "first class—you know
you deserve it." Woof-woof.

Another roar from the crowd.

UMPIRE Silence, please. The players have requested silence.

*Sound of an ace being served. Again we see Leona and Midge in
close-up on the monitors.*

RYAN (*in a low whisper*) Several viewers have called in. Kelly:
What's a Pittsburgh Incline conductor?

KELLY The Pittsburgh Incline is like a cable car, only it runs
on tracks, like a funicular, and it takes you to the top of the
bluff overlooking the city of Pittsburgh across the
Monongahela and Allegheny rivers.

RYAN That's a word you don't hear much anymore,
funicular.

KELLY Like the song: Finuculee, funicular!

RYAN Why didn't you say so? You've got a nice voice.

UMPIRE Advantage Sawallisch.

MIDGE It's turned out to be a lovely day. They were
predicting rain.

LEONA I knew it wasn't going to rain today. My left leg told me before I left the hotel.

MIDGE I hope you're not getting weird, Lee. The southwest does that to people. Chicky Chickering moved to Santa Fe to be with her grandchildren and became a massage therapist.

LEONA It beats sitting around rocking.

MIDGE She's our age! That's too old to be massaging people. They should be massaging us.

RYAN What do you think old friends like that talk about?

LEONA I can see her nipples!

KELLY I don't know but you can be sure they have a lot of ground to cover.

MIDGE A lot of them do that now.

LEONA What? Show their nipples?

MIDGE (*snapping her fingers*) You gotta get with it, Leona.

LEONA This is the worst part about getting old: the impotence. You're helpless to do anything. You can say all you want—but it's not the same thing.

RYAN What fascinates me is how these two women, once so active in the sport, spend their twilight years?

MIDGE It's their nipples.

KELLY Midge is a grandmother and an avid reader while Leona spends time coaching tennis with underprivileged youth.

RYAN Good for her. Tennis has had a bad rap as an elitist sport long enough.

LEONA It's very distracting.

MIDGE You're still so bossy.

LEONA That's not true. I have strong opinions and I express them.

MIDGE Unsolicited.

RYAN The future of this game—if it's going to have one—belongs to everyone. Take baseball and Jackie Robinson.

LEONA I also happen to be right more often than not and I think a woman's nipples are very distracting at a tennis match.

RYAN Otherwise, where are the next Venus and Serena gonna come from?

MIDGE I agree with you 100 percent.

Roar from the crowd.

RYAN Ooo! That was a tremendous crosscourt forehand from Lanvin-Grillet.

KELLY Sawallisch was lucky to even get a piece of it.

LEONA Then why aren't you sharing my outrage?

MIDGE I'm too old. In a little while, none of this will matter. My eye is on the long-term prize now, not some French girl's nipples. Let go, Lee. It's their turn.

LEONA The only thing I ever really cared about was tennis. How it was played. Who played it. Well, tennis and Kip.

MIDGE Why did you stop going to church?

LEONA One less thing to do.

MIDGE   I'd appreciate a less glib answer, Lee.

LEONA   I got tired of people looking at me when I went. "There's Leona Mullen. She looks terrible."

MIDGE   Have you lost your faith?

LEONA   I lost something.

MIDGE   It's a terrible thing to lose.

Sound of first serve and volley. They watch a while. Enormous response from crowd for a point well played.

UMPIRE   Deuce.

MIDGE   I'm very glad we came back for this.

LEONA   I almost didn't, you know.

MIDGE   That would have been so like you.

LEONA   Twice I unpacked my little valise.

MIDGE   You've always had trouble accepting any of the good stuff, I like to call it: appreciation, affection, gratitude.

LEONA   Judge my game; not, did you like me? Was I good at tennis? That's all I wanted to know.

MIDGE   You were very good at it, right up until our last match. September 27th, 1976, Forest Hills, our old stomping grounds.

LEONA   I hardly remember that day.

MIDGE   Consider that a blessing. I remember everything.

LEONA   Thirty-one years ago? We were ancient even then.

MIDGE   For tennis, we were decrepit. We came out of

retirement for it. It was an exhibition match against Ronald Woods and Rafael Vegas. One of those Battles of the Sexes.

LEONA We creamed them.

MIDGE I hate that expression.

LEONA You always did. Creamed! I love it. You don't have to speak English to know what it means. Creamed!

MIDGE Six-love, six-love. They didn't know what hit them. Of course, they were in their sixties and practically using walkers. The men said we intimidated them into defeat. We had the honor of our sex at stake and I think we both knew we'd never play together again.

LEONA Our last hurrah and we wasted it on a circus exhibition. That was the year Kip was killed.

MIDGE When we last played? Yes. What made you change your mind about coming today?

LEONA You didn't think I was going to let you have the last word on us?

MIDGE It would have been awful without you.

LEONA We'll exorcise our demons together. Give them what they came for.

MIDGE I never know when you're kidding.

LEONA That's alright, Midge, neither do I.

MIDGE I had my doubts, too, but the children were very insistent. "You can't say you've been forgotten, mother, if you don't show up."

LEONA How would you have explained my absence?

Sounds of a first serve.

MIDGE I would have told them the truth.

LEONA But you don't know the truth.

A roar from the crowd.

UMPIRE Game Sawallisch.

LEONA No! No, no, no. The French girl's backhand is going to be her downfall. Her racquet is never far enough back and the angle is too high. Down and up, not straight across.

MIDGE I bet you're a wonderful coach. I hope those teenagers appreciate you.

LEONA Probably not. But there's one I've got my eye on. She could be the real thing if she's willing to put in the hours. She's lazy.

MIDGE You've always had a marvelous eye for the weaknesses of others.

LEONA I simply found my opponent's weak spot and showed her no mercy.

MIDGE I preferred to psychologically wear them down. Remember what that writer for *The Times* called us? Brutal Finesse.

LEONA How could I forget? Brutal Finesse! Kip wanted to name the sailboat that: BRUTAL FINESSE. Over my dead body, you will, I told him.

MIDGE You always had that ferocious will to win.

LEONA So did you.

MIDGE With me it was more a steadfast *desire*. I was afraid to show the world the savage I might have become if I hadn't kept her carefully under wraps all those years.

LEONA   I was the savage for both of us. I didn't mind. In fact, I rather liked it.

MIDGE   I hid behind your fury at the net and did my genteel slicing and dicing from the base line.

LEONA   You know I've never gone back to the stables?

MIDGE   I don't wonder.

LEONA   I still own them, I just don't go. I see someone on horseback, especially if they're jumping, and I have to look away. Has any man ever been more elegant, more graceful, more athletic than Kip?

MIDGE   No, none.

LEONA   He'd spent his life with horses. How does such a thing happen? Why does a horse he loved all of a sudden balk? Why did someone who made me feel safe abandon me in an instant? It's all so arbitrary. You're here, you're there, you're gone. I've had thirty-one years to ask these questions and I still can't answer them.

Sounds of ball being served from stage left, then three return volleys with a huge crowd response.

LEONA (*cont.*)   Well done! What was her name again?

MIDGE   Giselle.

LEONA   Well done, Giselle! Keep it up, keep it up! Let's turn on some heat!

Sound of ball being served; Leona stands and watches the point being played.

MIDGE   The indomitable Leona Mullen! As *present*, as vibrant as ever but just as remote as well. Who is Leona? I don't know the truth, she said. I've never known the truth about her. But does anyone of us ever truly know another? I don't mean secrets. Secrets are easy to keep, they're nothing but little lies. Nobody cares I slept with Barbara Hastings' husband in Los Angeles in 1963. Two days later President Kennedy was shot. Our tawdry little secret was completely upstaged by American history. I could tell Leona I slept with Kip and Leona would get very angry, probably never speak to me again. It would be a lie but she would remember it for the rest of her life. It would have made her less remote—for that one terrible moment when I told her that I had slept with him. What a silly fantasy. What a crazy old woman I'm becoming; no, *become*. Then turn back from that direction. Stop that slide into the ridiculous. Heave to, come about, old girl, you can do it. It doesn't have to be like this.

The sound of a second service.

UMPIRE   Out! I agree with the call. I saw the ball out.

LEONA   Out? It was on the line! What does he mean, calling it out???

MIDGE   Cyclops would seem to agree with him. See? The ball's just over the line.

LEONA   Well it looked in to me.

MIDGE   Well it's not.

LEONA   That's not the point. Nobody stands a chance against a goddamn machine.

MIDGE You called a linesman in Berlin an asshole and we were fined five thousand deutsche marks.

LEONA I didn't know he spoke English. Give her hell, Giselle!

Sound of first serve. Volley ensues. Leona enjoys it hugely.

MIDGE You can be sure Leona isn't going to end in madness or self-pity. How eagerly she gives herself to this game she can't play anymore. With such passion she seizes things. She doesn't look, she devours.

Cheer from crowd.

MIDGE (*cont.*) She lives so fully in the moment because she cannot bear the past and is fearful of what lies ahead. But so am I. I have never felt closer to anyone than I do to you right now, Lee, but I have never felt more shut out from anyone as well.

Volley starts, then stops, cheer from crowd.

UMPIRE Advantage Sawallisch.

The lights return to "normal."

LEONA I'm switching back to the Czech girl. What kind of name is Lanvin-Grillet anyway?

MIDGE Is there anything about women's tennis that doesn't enrage you, Lee?

LEONA Did we have hyphenated names in our day?

MIDGE Martha Willis wanted to be called Martha Willis-Webster but it didn't stick.

LEONA That was because she was an unpleasant woman and a mediocre player. No one wanted to accommodate her.

MIDGE There was Evonne Goolagong-Cawley.

LEONA As if Evonne Goolagong weren't enough of a mouthful! We could have hyphenated our names but we had too much class. Martha Willis-Webster indeed!

MIDGE But you're happy with Alex? He's been a good husband?

LEONA I'm not thinking about hyphenating my name with his.

MIDGE I was hoping he'd come with you today.

LEONA This sort of thing isn't for him. He's still too busy. He says he's retired, but he's not. That man has a finger in every pie.

MIDGE He seems very nice.

LEONA He's very successful.

MIDGE Wildly, from what I gather.

LEONA Best of all, he's his own man. He says exactly what's on his mind and does exactly as he pleases. I think that's what I like best about him: His independence. It's given me mine. He's everything I could ask for in a husband. He's just not Kip.

MIDGE Well of course, he's not. No one could be Kip.

LEONA I always thought you were a little in love with Kip.

MIDGE Everyone was a little in love with him, Leona. Even the lesbians on the tour would have left their girlfriends for your husband.

LEONA I think some of the men would, too. He could have had anyone. He chose me.

MIDGE I remember what you said when you saw him in the parking lot at Forest Hills. He was getting into a green Chrysler convertible and you said, "That is the most attractive man I've ever seen."

LEONA It's true, he was.

MIDGE "Millionaire or pauper, lawyer or Indian chief, I'm going to marry him."

LEONA I didn't care what he was.

MIDGE Paupers weren't generally seen getting into Chrysler convertibles in the parking lot at the Forest Hills Tennis Club. Neither were Native American chiefs, for that matter. The girl from Pittsburgh married up and the Park Avenue debutante married down.

LEONA You didn't marry down. You married a son of a bitch.

MIDGE I didn't know that when I married him.

LEONA I had my suspicions.

MIDGE I wish you had shared them.

LEONA You were in love, you wouldn't have listened. God, we were both so young and lusty.

MIDGE I was never lusty.

LEONA You were, too.

MIDGE I was not.

LEONA You were, Midge.

MIDGE Well, not like you.

LEONA You had an affair with a black man.

MIDGE You mean Sam?

LEONA People didn't do things like that back then.

MIDGE It wasn't deliberate. I had no choice. He swept me off my feet.

LEONA The booing we got for a while, the catcalls.

MIDGE It strengthened my game.

LEONA It threw mine. We had a rotten season that year. I hated being booed, even though I knew it was you they were booing.

MIDGE I felt like Joan of Arc with a tennis racquet.

LEONA In the old days, you would have said *Jeanne d'Arc* with a tennis racquet.

MIDGE I think our pretensions fall away as we grow older.

LEONA Mine have only grown. You should hear me ordering a lobster for lunch in our condo clubhouse. I don't know who I think I'm impressing. The waiter? I'm usually eating by myself. Alex is off somewhere being Mr. Tucson.

UMPIRE Advantage, Lanvin-Grillet.

MIDGE Sam wrote me a couple of years ago. He said he and his wife would be passing through on their summer vacation and could they stop by?

LEONA You said yes?

MIDGE Of course I did. I wanted to see what she looked like. Besides, how many people are just "passing through" Blue Harbor?

LEONA I will never understand why you chose Maine when you had forty-nine other states.

MIDGE She was a lovely woman.

LEONA Was she black?

MIDGE Yes. It's such an odd word. So few are. She was a lovely cocoa butter. Very well-dressed. She was in a Chanel suit. I think that was to impress me. You don't drive halfway across country in a Chanel suit for nothing. She's dean of admissions at a very good girls' school in Evanston. Sam had gone on to be very successful in real estate: vacation homes for well-to-do black people. "Compounds" he called them.

LEONA Like the Kennedys, sort of Hyannisport for Negroes?

MIDGE I don't know if I'd put it like that, Lee...!

LEONA What did I say?

MIDGE You called them Negroes.

LEONA I was raised to say Negroes.

MIDGE If you want to date yourself!

LEONA It's a perfectly good word. Innocuous even, I'd call it.

MIDGE We had a very civilized lunch.

LEONA All right, African-American. There, I said it!

MIDGE I made my famous tuna salad for them.

LEONA I didn't say the N-word. You were always on my back about things like that.

MIDGE You should be thankful I was.

LEONA It was just words, never my heart.

MIDGE Words matter.

LEONA I didn't have your education. Or advantages. Or breeding. Finish your story.

MIDGE I could not tell for the life of me if Esther—that was her name—if Esther knew that her husband and I had been lovers.

LEONA I'm sure she did. The Chanel suit, you said so yourself.

MIDGE They seemed very happy. They're grandparents. They were on their way to Prince Edward Island to see one of their children and his family. It was as if Sam and I had never happened.

LEONA I remember the night he stood in the parking lot outside our motel room and shouted for you to come down to him and honked the horn and didn't stop until you did.

MIDGE He woke the whole hotel up.

LEONA I was more than a little jealous.

MIDGE You were already married to Kip!

LEONA Kip never woke up an entire motel for me.

MIDGE After lunch . . .

LEONA You still add the spicy pimento bits to the tuna?

MIDGE Of course I do.

LEONA Because without them . . !

MIDGE I'm touched you remember.

LEONA In Tucson I pass it off as my own recipe.

MIDGE I don't mind.

LEONA I wasn't asking if you minded. I was confessing.

MIDGE Consider yourself forgiven. Anyway, I was walking them out to their car . . .

LEONA And I was definitely not asking for your forgiveness.

LEONA Was it a Lexus?

MIDGE I don't know.

LEONA I bet it was. Rich African-Americans all drive Lexuses. Tucson is filled with wealthy, retired African-Americans in their Lexus's.

MIDGE Sometimes you leave me speechless, Lee.

LEONA What did I say? It's true.

MIDGE At the car, Sam touched my elbow for just a second, his wife didn't see the gesture, she was heading for her side of the car, and our eyes met and his look told me that he remembered every moment, every second of when we were together. I was suddenly very glad they came.

UMPIRE Game, Lanvin-Grillet.

LEONA You should have married Ben Beeson. You could be living on Park Avenue, not some backwater in Maine.

MIDGE Blue Harbor is very beautiful.

LEONA Kip and I were so angry when Paul left you.

MIDGE The children were angrier. They still are and he's been dead eleven years now.

LEONA I heard the cunt was living in Cannes now with that man who writes those books they make all those spy movies out of.

MIDGE She is but it's Capri and I wish you wouldn't use that word.

LEONA She took your husband. That's a very cunt-like thing to do, Midge. I saw one of the movies on a plane once. It was actually rather good. I forgot how much I hated flying.

MIDGE You always liked anything with espionage.

LEONA I felt disloyal to you.

MIDGE That's ridiculous. The cunt didn't write it. I think a man who falls in love with another woman and leaves his wife and family for her without a word to any of them—especially the children—is very, very weak.

LEONA Why especially the children?

MIDGE We bring them into this world through no fault or wish of their own and then we involve them in the terrible messes we've made of our lives.

LEONA But yours have turned out all right, haven't they?

MIDGE All right is never a mother's wish. I was hoping for something more. Like we had, Lee.

LEONA I know.

MIDGE Were we really better than most people?

LEONA When we played good tennis, yes, I think we were.

MIDGE Why were we blessed and our children weren't? I just hope they're happy. Remember Ted Lewis and his band? He'd periodically call out to us on the dance floor: "Is everybody happy?" Now the question is: "Is anybody happy?"

LEONA It takes very little to make me happy. When I'm regular I'm on cloud nine.

MIDGE When I'm regular I'm on cloud twenty.

LEONA I've got something for that.

MIDGE I'm sure I'm already taking it. They've got me on something for everything.

LEONA Still, we're not too poorly off for a couple of old birds.

Sound of ball being served, volley.

ADMIRER These two young players are terrific. They can do it all: serve, volley, charge the net or play power tennis from the baseline. There's no question: they are both excellent, superb even, tennis players.

UMPIRE Game, Sawallisch.

ADMIRER Still, I can't give my heart to these two the way I lost it to Leona Mullen and Margaret Barker all those years ago. Why can't I distinguish them from the two young women who played a quarter-finals match at this same stadium at the U.S. Open last year? One of them defeated the other but I don't remember who they were. The first time I saw Leona Mullen and Margaret Barker all those years ago is still more vivid than this match being played today. You and I play tennis. Leona Mullen and Midge Barker did something else. They were artists we could imagine knowing. They were you and me, only better. Maybe that's why I don't have as much invested in who wins at tennis anymore. It's their fault.

KELLY Did you ever play much doubles, Ryan?

RYAN Doubles never much appealed to me. I don't think I had the right ego for it. You've got to love your partner to be good at doubles. Frankly, I was too worried about my own game to worry about someone else's. His mistakes are yours and vice versa.

KELLY I think doubles was a whole other game in their day. You played it because you wanted to. It was its own sport. Now it's more something you do between singles matches.

RYAN We might get a little argument there.

KELLY Who from?

RYAN Our guests of honor.

ANNOUNCER Is there a doctor in the stands? Is there a doctor?

LEONA Someone must have taken ill. They've stopped playing.

ANNOUNCER We have someone in Section D, in a courtside box, who needs immediate attention. May we have a doctor, please!

MIDGE There, see? They're all crowding around someone.

LEONA They shouldn't do that. That's the first thing they tell you: don't crowd around the person!

MIDGE It looks like a woman. She's not that old.

LEONA Oh, God, don't die on us! Don't die, don't die, don't die!

MIDGE Everything's going to be fine, Lee. Look, here comes someone down the steps. She must be a doctor.

LEONA I hope they've called for an ambulance.

MIDGE She looks like she knows what she's doing.

LEONA I could have become a doctor just as easily as a tennis player and been saving someone's life right now instead of retired and completely useless.

MIDGE She's sitting up.

Applause from the crowd for the woman.

LEONA Thank God.

MIDGE Look! She's waving to the crowd. She's fine, Lee.

LEONA Why is it when we're hurt or injured we're so quick to pretend we're not?

MIDGE It's human nature.

LEONA I played half a set in Monterrey with a torn calf muscle and even you didn't know.

MIDGE You didn't tell me until we got to the locker room.

LEONA If we all went around letting everyone know how much pain we were in, we wouldn't have time for anything else. There wouldn't be doctors *or* tennis players. Just people taking care of one another.

UMPIRE Resume play.

LEONA They haven't even taken her away yet.

MIDGE They will.

LEONA They could have waited until she was gone.

MIDGE Life goes on, Lee.

LEONA Sometimes I wish it wouldn't. That it would just stop and we could all take a good look at it and have a good cry.

That's all: a good cry and then we'd all pull our socks up and get on with it.

MIDGE   What do you want to cry about?

LEONA   All of it—well, nearly all of it. It goes by so fast and we understand so little.

MIDGE   Maybe we're not supposed to.

LEONA   Where is the son of a bitch buried?

MIDGE   He was cremated. And please stop calling him that. He was my husband and the father of my children. The cunt threw his ashes into the Bay of Naples.

LEONA   I believe the expression is "scattered".

MIDGE   Not where she's concerned. Believe me, she threw them. Are you going to hate dying?

LEONA   Yes. And I'm trying very hard not to. It's a ridiculous thing to be afraid of when you think about it.

MIDGE   Not so ridiculous.

LEONA   Animals aren't afraid of dying. They just get on with it. You know, I'm doing yoga—

MIDGE   You are not!

LEONA   I am. Why do you find that so surprising?

MIDGE   You used to hate anything good for you.

LEONA   That's a goddamn lie. Let me finish, just once! There's a pose at the end of yoga called *savasana,* which means "corpse" or "dead man's" pose. You just lie there and sink into the floor. Your breathing gets very still. You don't think you can ever move again. Everything stops but your mind and that's what I'm afraid death is: being alive in your mind but nowhere else. And that will be eternity: just lying there, unable to move, thinking, thinking, thinking, and not being able to do anything about it. Not being able to tell someone you love them or forgive them or tell them something nice even: "That's a nice dress. You've changed your hair." You've run out of chances. When I think about it, I become so anxious I can't breathe.

We hear the sound of an ambulance approaching.

LEONA (*cont.*)   Finally! I hope they take her to a good hospital.

MIDGE   I'm afraid of dying because of the pain involved.

LEONA   There doesn't have to be pain.

MIDGE   There is always pain.

LEONA   You don't know that.

MIDGE   How could there not be? They just tell us there isn't.

LEONA   Kip wasn't in pain at the end.

At no response from Midge.

LEONA (*cont.*)   You don't believe that?

MIDGE   It's not important what I believe.

LEONA   Maybe they should take us out behind some barn and shoot us.

MIDGE   Good idea. Does your condo have a barn?

LEONA   No.

MIDGE   Neither does mine.

UMPIRE   Game Sawallisch. Four all.

MIDGE I was doing my morning walk last week and there was a station wagon loaded with vacation things—bicycles, tents. It was going very slowly. I heard a child's voice coming from inside. "Good-bye, good-bye, everybody," she was calling out, over and over. She sounded quite happy about it. "Good-bye, everybody, good-bye." It was the loveliest thing. "Good-bye, good-bye, everybody." What a way to end a vacation. "Good-bye, good-bye, everyone." I started crying. That's how I want to go.

She turns to Leona.

MIDGE (*cont.*) Lee, I didn't tell you that Kip was in pain.

LEONA Whether he was or he wasn't, he's gone. What you believe or what they told me has very little to do with it.

Sounds of ambulance driving away.

LEONA (*cont.*) Godspeed, stranger.

MIDGE I said a little prayer for her and I'm not sure I believe in God.

LEONA What do you believe in? Is there a name for it?

There is a cheer from the crowd.

MIDGE Goodwill.

LEONA What? I missed that.

MIDGE Goodwill.

LEONA Oh. Goodwill.

MIDGE It's the source of my faith, such as it is.

LEONA I'm going to miss these young women dressed like

advertisements competing for major cash prizes that were not available to our generation.

MIDGE I'm going to miss everything about it.

LEONA I think the game will remember us.

MIDGE When I was younger, I wanted to live forever. The sad thing is I still do.

LEONA Have you given any thought to where you want to be buried?

MIDGE I'm going up the chimney like Paul. I don't know what they do with your ashes in Blue Harbor. Put them in a lobster trap, I suppose. You?

LEONA I've asked to be buried next to my parents.

MIDGE Not with Kip?

LEONA Kip knew how much I loved him. I don't think my parents did. I don't expect anyone to come to the funeral. It's Pittsburgh, for Christ's sake.

MIDGE I'll be there.

LEONA I'm not coming to Blue Harbor for yours.

MIDGE There won't be one. Straight up the chimney, I told you.

LEONA I'm sure I'll go before you.

MIDGE You don't know that.

LEONA Yes, yes I do.

MIDGE That's lovely, Leona, being buried with your parents.

LEONA I adored them, especially my mother. I don't think my father noticed me when I didn't have a racquet in my hand.

MIDGE I hardly knew mine. The way people talk to one another today, the way we're talking—we never did that. They never understood what this game meant to me.

UMPIRE Deuce.

LEONA The older you get, the easier it is to be honest. I don't care if people like me anymore.

MIDGE You've been saying that your whole life.

LEONA Now I mean it.

MIDGE I never thought you liked me.

LEONA That's ridiculous.

MIDGE The way people like to be liked. Need to be.

LEONA Nonsense.

MIDGE Well, there it is. I'm glad I said it.

LEONA Why didn't you say something?

MIDGE I just did.

LEONA I meant then.

MIDGE We were a good team. We were two for the books. That's all that mattered.

LEONA I never realized how much you disliked me.

MIDGE I didn't dislike you, Lee. You disappointed me.

LEONA You've waited thirty years to tell me that?

MIDGE It doesn't matter. We won Wimbledon and danced with Cary Grant.

LEONA That's cold consolation for what we're talking about, Midge.

MIDGE Consolation, nonetheless.

UMPIRE Game, Sawallisch. Five games all.

LEONA Do you remember the first time we met?

MIDGE It was the only time we ever played one another. You creamed me.

LEONA I thought you hated that word.

MIDGE Consider it a gift.

LEONA I didn't exactly cream you. The first set was seven-five. The second set you fell apart, it's true: six-love.

MIDGE The final game of the first set was the turning point. We stayed at deuce for what seemed like hours. The advantage went back and forth between us point after point after point.

LEONA I loathe deuce.

MIDGE I know, Lee.

LEONA It's so undecisive. I'd rather lose than be stuck at deuce. After all the work and effort of the first six points, you're right back where you started. "Why are you still there?" I wanted to shout at our opponents across the net. I think the look I gave them when we were at deuce did the trick: "You're going down this time, ladies."

MIDGE I always found deuce rather exciting. You're standing on the brink of utter triumph or complete annihilation.

LEONA We didn't win championships all those years staying at deuce. We won them going for the jugular. We lost the Australian because we stayed at deuce too long. Eleven times we went back to deuce from match point. The twelfth time they had the advantage. You were playing brilliantly. It was my serve. And this time, just before I threw the ball up in the air, I said to myself, "I'm going to toss this ball so high Midge won't have anything to say about it back in the clubhouse. And then I'm going to hit it so hard and at such an angle, she will think to herself: "That was the greatest serve in the history of women's tennis." And then, I double-faulted.

MIDGE You put too much pressure on yourself.

LEONA No, I double-faulted. The Melbourne papers ran a photo of me: the ball is being tossed with one hand—great extension—and the racquet is nicely back in the other. It's a classic tennis photo. The headline above it read: PERFECT FORM, BITTER OUTCOME. If you look at my eyes in the photo, you see the terror of being at match point.

MIDGE Let it go, Lee, I have.

LEONA Don't patronize me, Midge. I apologized to you.

MIDGE I didn't want your apology. You were more important to me than a game.

LEONA I cost you the Grand Slam.

MIDGE You cost me nothing, Leona. You cost yourself.

LEONA Then why did you quit?

MIDGE I didn't want to continue playing a game I loved with a partner who couldn't accept my forgiveness for her double fault.

LEONA I lost everything I loved—first tennis, then Kip.

MIDGE Oh, Lee!

LEONA We said we weren't going to do this.

MIDGE You should have gotten another partner.

LEONA I didn't want another partner. I wanted another chance to win the Australian.

MIDGE I always wondered why you chose to play doubles with a woman you never really liked. People always said you could have been the greatest singles player in the history of women's tennis.

LEONA I wanted to be the greatest but I didn't dare to find out. I dislike myself for that. Didn't you ever want to be the greatest?

MIDGE I wanted to be the best I could.

LEONA And what if that wasn't the greatest?

MIDGE Together we were the greatest doubles players in the history of women's tennis. That has to count for something, Lee.

LEONA I don't believe in choices. Things happen because we let them happen and we let happen what we want to happen. And I let this happen.

MIDGE We're at deuce. Don't you want to hit a winner?

LEONA Not anymore. Do you?

MIDGE I'd rather watch these two.

LEONA Me, too.

Sound of serve, volley.

LEONA (*cont.*)   You lucky, lucky young women. You have your whole lives ahead of you to play tennis.

A huge sound from the crowd.

RYAN   Tremendous tennis!

KELLY   I'd stopped breathing!

RYAN   That just might have been the most exciting point of the entire match.

KELLY   Whatever it was, it's gotten us to match point.

LEONA   It *is* a nail-biter.

MIDGE   My money's on California.

LEONA   I'll stick with The Frog. I did like you, Midge.

MIDGE   Thank you, Leona. I liked you, too. Shhhhh!

Sounds of a first service. Groans of disappointment from the crowd.

UMPIRE   Second serve.

KELLY   Can she hold her serve?

RYAN   Can she hold her nerve?

Scream from crowd.

UMPIRE   Ladies and gentlemen. Quiet, please!

LEONA   It all goes so fast.

MIDGE   Too fast.

LEONA   And for what?

MIDGE   For this.

Sounds of second serve. Player who double-faulted screams. Crowd reacts.

LEONA She double-faulted!

UMPIRE Game, set and match.

The stadium applauds for the victorious player.

RYAN A double fault! That's a helluva way to win a match.

KELLY It's a worse way to lose one!

UMPIRE Ladies and Gentlemen. Ladies and Gentlemen.

LEONA I think this is us.

UMPIRE Ladies and Gentlemen, may I have your attention.

UMPIRE We are honored here today with the presence of two all-time tennis greats. I'm talking about none other than Leona Mullen and Margaret "Midge" Barker.

This time the stadium erupts in a huge ovation. Midge and Leona stand and acknowledge it. It takes a long time for the crowd to settle down.

MIDGE Thank you.

LEONA Yes, thank you.

MIDGE I'm Midge Mullen.

LEONA No, you're not. You're Midge *Barker* and I'm Leona Mullen, your old partner.

MIDGE I get very nervous when I have to speak in public. That's why I wrote something out.

LEONA They don't want to hear that, Midge.

MIDGE You don't?

Laughter from the fans.

LEONA Is there anybody out there who actually saw us play together?

A COUPLE OF VOICES Yes! We love you! You're still the greatest!

LEONA There is?

MIDGE We were pretty good, weren't we?

The crowd roars.

LEONA I just want to say to the young woman who double-faulted. Where is she? There you are! I double-faulted once. It became the story of my life. Don't let it become yours. . Thank you. My oldest friend, Midge Barker.

Applause. She hands the mike to Midge.

MIDGE Tennis is a wonderful sport. I am very glad I gave my life to it. More importantly is what it gave to me. A sense of family, a sense of accomplishment. When Lee and I played well, you were there for us. When we didn't, there was only your disappointment and never your blame. I can't begin to tell you what that has meant, today more than ever. We stand here in the tall shadows of the great women players who preceded us.

LEONA Dorothea Douglass Chambers! Suzanne Lenglen! Althea Gibson! Doris Hart! Who am I leaving out?

MIDGE Helen Wills Moody.

LEONA Helen Wills Moody! Bow down when I say their names!

MIDGE And I just want to say to all you young women to come: welcome. We wish you well.

LEONA Already you play better than any of us did.

MIDGE So thank you. All of you. And most of all you, Lee. You were a good partner. I couldn't have asked for anything more.

LEONA (*waving to the fans*) See you at next year's Open!

Cheers from crowd.

MIDGE You're crying.

LEONA I am not crying.

They continue to wave to the fans. We see them in close-up on the monitors.

RYAN You gotta hand it to 'em, Kelly.

KELLY Real class, no doubt about it, tennis royalty.

RYAN I'll say one thing for their generation of tennis.

KELLY What's that, Ryan?

RYAN When they played, it was for love of the game. It wasn't for the big bucks or the endorsements. It was tennis for tennis' sake.

Midge and Leona continue to accept the crowd's ovation as the lights begin to fade.

RYAN (*cont.*) Who's up next?

KELLY We have the new Wonder from Down Under versus The Next Great American Hope. It's going to be a real match.

The sounds are fading. Midge and Leona wave and hold hands from their place in the stands and also on the television monitor.

AN ADMIRER Look at them. This time really look. You will not see their likes again.

Blackout.

End of Play